THE
WORKWEEK
LUNCH
COOKBOOK

THE
WORKWEEK
LUNCH
COOKBOOK

Easy, Delicious Meals to **Meal Prep**, **Pack**
and **Take On the Go**

Talia Koren
Founder of **WORKWEEK LUNCH** ✗

PAGE STREET
PUBLISHING CO.

PAGE STREET
PUBLISHING CO.

For the
Workweek Lunch Community

CONTENTS

THE MEAL PREP LUNCH LOW DOWN

Do you want to enjoy home-cooked meals without actually cooking every day? Me too. And that's exactly what this book will help you accomplish.

Meal prep, also known as make-ahead meals or batch cooking, is the best approach to home-cooking if you don't want to cook and clean every day, but want to eat nutrient-dense, delicious meals frequently. It makes the food you want to eat during the week—or whenever you're busiest—more accessible.

I started meal prepping lunches for work right after college, when I moved into my own New York City apartment and quickly realized how expensive it was to support myself on an entry-level salary. Before learning to meal prep, I had a habit of spending $12 on lunch almost every day at work, which quickly added up. Eventually, I figured out that I could make the same meals I spent $60 per week on at home for much less, and I could customize them to my preferences and needs. The only catch was spending a few hours on Sundays cooking to make it happen, which was made more enjoyable by binge-watching *Game of Thrones* during the cooking process.

Early on in my meal prep journey, I got comments from coworkers about my food daily. They'd walk by my desk at lunchtime, see the food in my containers, and say: "Wow, that looks amazing, I wish I could do that," or ask, "How do you make such amazing lunches every week?" At the time, I knew I wanted to start a side hustle outside of my nine-to-five job as a writer for an online publication. I decided to combine my meal prep, writing and photography skills into a business where I could teach others how to create a solid system to make lunches for work.

In 2016, I started Workweek Lunch as a blog and Instagram account, which grew to over 100,000 followers in 18 months. By 2018, I launched an online meal plan subscription service to help my community make meal prep even easier, and I made Workweek Lunch my full-time job. Now, Workweek Lunch helps thousands of people all over the world meal prep to save time, money and energy with our subscription, The Workweek Lunch Meal Prep Program, as well as our free resources on the blog, and now this cookbook! While growing Workweek Lunch into the business it is today, I've tried dozens of different meal prep methods and hundreds of different recipes to figure out what works for meal prep and what doesn't.

In the first year of meal prepping lunches for work, I saved about $250 per month and finally felt like I had my food spending under control. Of course, there are more benefits to meal prepping than just the savings!

I love meal prep because of the instant gratification factor. Yes, it takes work upfront, but there's nothing more satisfying than opening the fridge on a Monday morning to find stacks of containers full of delicious home-cooked food to enjoy all week. Meal prepping gives us back the time we would normally spend cooking. It allows us to sleep longer in the morning before work, enjoy more of our lunch hour and spend more time relaxing after work instead of doing dishes.

It's also an amazing way to save money and reduce waste because you're more likely to use up entire vegetables when cooking big batch meals. All the recipes in this book were developed to not only taste delicious after a few days in the fridge, but to also avoid letting perishable ingredients go to waste, like greens and half-used canned ingredients that usually get left behind.

Most importantly, meal prep gives us peace of mind. There's such a strong feeling of security when you know you don't have to worry about what to do for lunch when you already have so many other decisions to make throughout the day. Meal prep is all about taking care of your future self.

In this book, you'll learn the best ways to make, store and reheat work lunches and tips for making meal plans you can stick to. And of course, you'll make delicious work meals that will satisfy you— and that your coworkers will be jealous of!

The Food Philosophy Behind Workweek Lunch

At Workweek Lunch, we embrace an Intuitive Eating approach to food. I believe we can eat healthy food that tastes great and separate that from weight loss. Intuitive Eating was developed by dietitians Evelyn Tribole and Elyse Resch to help people heal their relationship with food after years of dieting and weight cycling.

There are ten principles to Intuitive Eating to help us learn to make food decisions based on internal hunger and fullness cues, accessibility, practicality, gentle nutrition and joy in eating, rather than the external food rules that diets are generally made up of, which tend to be restrictive. You can learn more about Intuitive Eating on workweeklunch.com. Intuitive Eating is not a weight loss method. You can still practice Intuitive Eating if you have allergies or medical dietary restrictions, which is very different from restricting food for weight loss.

While the recipes in this book include a balance of protein, fat, carbohydrates and a variety of easy-to-find vegetables and fruits, they are not designed to be used for weight loss. There are no calories or macronutrients listed in these recipes.

One of the most common misconceptions about meal prep is that it's only used for weight loss. Not here! I prefer to teach folks to use meal prep as a tool to get more out of life, whether it's carving out more time in the workweek, saving money for what's more important or helping us have more energy to do what we love!

How To Use This Book

All of the recipes in this book are made to be meal prepped for three or four work lunches for one person, depending on the recipe. You can cook these recipes as meal prepped lunches or one-off dinners too. I believe lunch and dinner recipes are interchangeable! If cooking for two, see my tips below for couples meal planning.

When it comes to choosing recipes for meal prepped lunches and dinners, choose based on how many meals you will need for the first few days of the week. Every week is different, so look at your calendar to be aware of events, trips, dinners, dates, lunch meetings, etc. to plan around. I never recommend prepping for the entire week because life happens and you might have to skip a meal or not be in the mood for the meal you prepped— more on that later. I've been doing this long enough to know that it's always the case, so it's best to cook slightly fewer meals than you think you will need to avoid wasting food.

When I lived alone, I chose two recipes to cook each Sunday, which gave me three lunches and three dinners for the week. This system gave me the security of having meals prepped ahead without wasting food if a friend spontaneously wanted to get dinner or if we had lunch catered at work.

Prepping three servings of a meal gives you the ability to push them to another day or freeze them, if needed. When I cooked for two, I prepped recipes on a Sunday, which gave us nine to twelve meals depending on the recipe. Remember, meal prep isn't all or nothing! No matter how many people I'm prepping for, it's important to make room for eating out and throwing random dinners together during the week too.

If you're just starting out with meal prep for yourself, choose one recipe to make for a few work lunches and see how it goes. From there, you can build up to cooking more recipes on your meal prep day as needed.

If you're cooking for one and you're a veteran meal-prepper, make two or three recipes on your prep day. It's nice to have two options!

Are you cooking for yourself and a partner? Choose two recipes if you're only prepping lunches and three or four if you'd rather have lunches and dinners prepped ahead. Alternatively, you can double the recipes instead of choosing many different ones. Typically, variety is important, which is why prepping fewer portions of more recipes may be a better option than doubling these recipes. Check out my tips on making meal prep faster since meal prepping for two people definitely takes longer!

Whether you're cooking for one or two, it's better to prep fewer meals on Sunday than to have to toss food at the end of the week that you couldn't get to. Another tip would be to focus on freezer meals—we have an entire chapter on them! So if you can't finish every meal you made, you can at least save them for another week.

If you do happen to get bored of or tired of a meal you prepped—it will eventually happen, no matter how delicious the meal is—I've got your back! You can check out ideas for repurposing meal preps on page 29.

Here's the schedule I recommend: Choose the meals you want to make for the next week on Friday. Consider how many meals you need or want, what you're in the mood for and what's in your pantry or freezer already—this helps save money. Make your grocery list based on the meals you choose. On Saturday, shop for groceries. Then on Sunday, prep the meals you selected and shopped for! Avoid trying to choose meals, shop, cook and clean all on the same day. You'll be exhausted!

Meal planning is a really important aspect of getting meal prep right. You can find instructions on making your own meal plans on page 12 or use the sample meal plans I provide in this book. Get more meal planning resources and grocery lists at workweeklunch.com/cookbookguide. Without a meal plan, grocery shopping and meal prepping is a hundred times harder and you're more likely to waste food and money. Don't skip this crucial step!

Time-Saving Meal Prep Hacks

Meal prep involves frontloading the work in the kitchen so you can sit back and enjoy the gift of free time and stress-free meals throughout the week. The only catch is that you have to carve out time on your days off to make it happen!

It's no secret that meal prep takes time. But it doesn't have to take up an entire day. The average cook can expect to spend 2 to 3 hours on meal prep when cooking a few recipes for one. If cooking a few different recipes for two or more, the average cook can expect to spend 3 to 5 hours meal prepping. Find some tips and tricks for making meal prep faster on the next page.

MEAL PREP TIPS AND TRICKS

- If your budget allows, grab pre-chopped fresh or frozen ingredients at the supermarket. Any time you can save yourself during the chopping process will help make your meal prep sessions faster. Having super-sharp knives helps too!

- Choose meals that allow for easy multitasking. I like to strategically choose a meal that I can cook in the oven while I cook another meal on the stove. Hands-free meals like casseroles and soups make multitasking easy. Plus, they're easy to make big batches of. For example, you can make the Broccoli Cheddar Soup (page 43) on the stove while roasting up the Salmon & Sweet Potato Sheet Pan (page 36) in the oven.

- Make a meal prep plan like the ones you'll find in the next couple pages. After selecting your meals, read through the recipes to see what needs to be done first so you're not waiting around for an ingredient to cool down or soak before using it. Write down your plan on a piece of paper and stick it to your fridge. This also helps keep you from feeling overwhelmed when making multiple dishes.

- Always chop and prep your ingredients for every meal before you start to cook. If your schedule allows, chop ingredients the day or night before your meal prep day. Having every ingredient ready to go will make cooking multiple meals much smoother.

- Meal prep also goes by a lot faster when you're having fun! Throw on some comfy clothes, queue up a podcast and grab your favorite beverage. This isn't just prepping meals for the week—it's time for yourself too!

Make Meal Plans You'll Actually Stick To

The most successful meal preps start with a meal plan. To truly reap all the money and time-saving benefits of meal prep, I recommend making a quick plan on pen and paper, in Microsoft Excel—my favorite—or in the notes app on your phone! Meal planning also makes grocery list writing and shopping a breeze. The goal is to make a meal plan each week with meal preps you'll look forward to eating so that you'll actually stick to it!

When I first started meal planning, I tried to eat as "clean" as possible. It never worked because the meals were bland and sad. I also felt a sense of failure when I couldn't stick to these boring meal plans, and the food ended up in the trash. Finally, I ditched clean eating to focus on planning and cooking food that I love. Planning balanced and healthy meals is important to me, but I try not to obsess over nutrition. It's made meal planning and prepping more fun and realistic! I encourage you to trust that your meal preps will be as healthy and nourishing as you need them to be. Be realistic about what you truly like to eat and how much.

The other aspect of making meal plans you'll stick to is being honest with yourself about how much planned food you'll eat. I recommend under-planning a bit. Instead of planning twenty-one meals (three meals a day for seven days), plan your "struggle" meals (the meals that make you feel drained to think about in the moment) and let the rest be spontaneous. For me, this was lunch. I didn't want to have to stop my flow at work just to figure out a meal every single day. That's what inspired me to create Workweek Lunch! My plans are based around making sure I have lunches covered, but I leave dinners and breakfasts more open.

Expect life to happen too. Let's say you plan five lunches for the week, but then a friend spontaneously wants to try a new spot for lunch during work. That usually means you'll have to toss a meal to accommodate your new (and way more exciting) lunch plan. I recommend planning meals through Wednesday or Thursday in the work week, expecting meals to get pushed when life happens. That way, you don't waste food or feel guilty for changing your plans.

Sample Meal Plans

Here are five meal plans based on different dietary needs you can use that feature recipes in this book for lunches and dinners. They don't include breakfasts, as I find that many people prefer to keep breakfast open and whip something up quickly before work—avocado toast isn't exactly meal prep friendly! If you do want meal prep breakfast recipes, we have hundreds in the Workweek Lunch Meal Prep Program, which is our meal plan subscription. Even though this cookbook and these recipes are primarily used for work lunches, I've

included dinners in these plans from this book so you can see how to meal prep and get more variety.

To make these plans work, I suggest grocery shopping on the day before you plan on cooking. Cook every meal on your prep day, usually Sunday, and store individual portions in containers in the fridge until you're ready to eat and the freezer for extra servings. See the next section for my container recommendations and best practices for storing meals (page 27). Note that every recipe in this book and these plans include storage and reheating instructions. Then, all you have to do is heat up your meals and enjoy throughout the week!

Each meal plan includes a freezer meal so that you can pop servings to eat on Thursday and Friday in the freezer on Sunday after you cook them. This method helps you avoid having to worry about meals lasting from Sunday to Friday, which can be a stretch. It also cuts down the need to cook and do dishes during the week, which is always a bonus! In addition to a freezer meal, I like to include a fast and easy meal that can be made in one pot or requires minimal cooking, a no-reheat meal in case you're on the go and don't have access to a microwave and one meal that's just a little more labor-intensive, but 100 percent worth it.

Lastly, these meal plans are designed around making sure you get a variety of macronutrients! One of the hallmarks of a good meal plan is using different proteins, veggies and carb elements so you don't get bored. Repetition is one of the biggest barriers of meal prep, and my goal is to show you that you don't have to eat the same meals over and over to make meal prep work. Yes, you have to be okay with some repetition to enjoy meal prep, but if you make meals you really love and look forward to, you'll want to eat them a few times!

Vegan 5-Day Workweek Meal Plan

Lunch	Chipotle Black Bean Avocado Quinoa Salad (page 54)	Butternut Squash Chickpea Kale Salad (page 80)	Chipotle Black Bean Avocado Quinoa Salad (page 54)	Lentil Butternut Squash Coconut Curry (page 124)	Lentil Butternut Squash Coconut Curry (page 124)
Dinner	Butternut Squash Chickpea Kale Salad (page 80)	Chipotle Black Bean Avocado Quinoa Salad (page 54)	Butternut Squash Chickpea Kale Salad (page 80)	OPEN	OPEN

TIPS

- You can use the butternut squash in both the salad and the curry.

- You'll have four total servings of the lentil curry. Store them all in the freezer on your prep day, enjoy two for this week's plan and save the remaining two for another busy week!

- Keep extra tortillas on hand in case you want to turn either salad into a wrap.

- On prep day, chop everything you need for the three recipes first, starting with the butternut squash salad recipe, since everything needs to cool. Then, cook the curry recipe and finally, the quinoa salad recipe.

Grocery List

Pink = Chipotle Black Bean Avocado Quinoa Salad (page 54)

Blue = Butternut Squash Chickpea Kale Salad (page 80)

Green = Lentil Butternut Squash Coconut Curry (page 124)

Black = Overlapping ingredients

PRODUCE

- [ ] 2 limes (1 for the quinoa salad, 1 for the curry)
- [ ] 2 cups (32 g) cilantro (1 cup [16 g] for the curry, 1 cup [16 g] for the quinoa salad)
- [ ] 1 butternut squash (½ for the kale salad, ½ for the curry)
- [ ] 1 lemon
- [ ] 1 cup (186 g) cherry tomatoes
- [ ] ⅔ cup (96 g) chopped red onion
- [ ] 3 radishes
- [ ] 3 cups (100 g) spinach
- [ ] 3 scallions
- [ ] 1 avocado
- [ ] 4 cups (268 g) chopped kale
- [ ] 1 honeycrisp apple
- [ ] ½ cup (80 g) chopped yellow onion

PANTRY

- [ ] ½ cup (120 ml) olive oil (divided among all the recipes)
- [ ] ⅔ cup (112 g) quinoa
- [ ] 1⅓ cups (320 ml) vegetable broth (sub water)
- [ ] 1 (15-oz [420-ml]) can black beans, rinsed and drained
- [ ] 2 chipotle peppers in adobo sauce and 3 tsp (15 ml) of adobo sauce
- [ ] 2 tbsp (30 ml) mayonnaise
- [ ] Tortilla chips, for serving
- [ ] Cooking spray
- [ ] ¼ cup (60 ml) maple syrup
- [ ] 1 (15-oz [425-ml]) can chickpeas, rinsed and drained
- [ ] ⅔ cup (92 g) pepitas

- [ ] 1 tbsp (6 g) red curry paste
- [ ] 1 (15-oz [420-ml]) can fire-roasted crushed tomatoes
- [ ] 1 cup (192 g) dry red or brown lentils
- [ ] 1 (15-oz [420-ml]) can coconut milk
- [ ] 1 cup (200 g) rice
- [ ] ¼ cup (60 ml) honey
- [ ] ¼ cup (60 ml) Dijon mustard
- [ ] 1 tbsp (15 ml) Worcestershire or soy sauce

SPICES

- [ ] Salt and pepper
- [ ] 1 tsp chili powder
- [ ] 1 tsp garlic powder (sub 2 cloves garlic)
- [ ] ½ tsp allspice
- [ ] ½ tsp paprika
- [ ] 3 tsp (8 g) cumin
- [ ] 1 tsp curry powder
- [ ] ½ tsp cinnamon
- [ ] 1½ tsp (4 g) garam masala
- [ ] 1 tsp turmeric
- [ ] ¼ tsp crushed red pepper flakes, optional

Vegetarian 5-Day Workweek Meal Plan

Lunch	Thai-Inspired Tofu Chopped Salad (page 83)	Kimchi Veggie Fried Rice (page 96)	Thai-Inspired Tofu Chopped Salad (page 83)	Veggie Chili Mac 'N' Cheese (page 119)	Veggie Chili Mac 'N' Cheese (page 119)
Dinner	Kimchi Veggie Fried Rice (page 96)	Thai-Inspired Tofu Chopped Salad (page 83)	Kimchi Veggie Fried Rice (page 96)	OPEN	OPEN

TIPS

- Any leftover vegetables from the Thai salad can go in the kimchi fried rice or chili mac.

- You'll have four total servings of the chili mac. Store them all in the freezer on your prep day, enjoy two for this week's plan and save the remaining two for another busy week!

- On prep day, get the tofu for the salad going before making the rice for the fried rice so it can cool. Make the chili mac, finish the Thai salad and then make the kimchi fried rice last.

Grocery List

Pink = Thai-Inspired Tofu Chopped Salad (page 83)

Blue = Kimchi Veggie Fried Rice (page 96)

Green = Veggie Chili Mac 'N' Cheese (page 119)

Black = Overlapping ingredients

PRODUCE

- [ ] 2½ cups (175 g) shredded or chopped red cabbage (1½ cups [105 g] for the salad, 1 cup [70 g] for the fried rice)
- [ ] 5 cloves garlic (divided among all the recipes)
- [ ] 1½ yellow onion (½ for the fried rice, 1 for the chili mac)
- [ ] 6 scallions (3 for the fried rice, 3 for the chili mac)
- [ ] 1 red bell pepper
- [ ] 2 carrots
- [ ] 4 cups (288 g) romaine lettuce
- [ ] 1 cup (16 g) chopped cilantro
- [ ] 1-inch (2.5-cm) piece ginger
- [ ] 2 limes
- [ ] 2 cups (226 g) shiitake mushrooms
- [ ] 2 cups (166 g) snap peas
- [ ] 1 poblano pepper, chopped

PANTRY

- [ ] ½ cup (120 ml) soy sauce (¼ cup [60 ml] for the fried rice, ¼ cup [60 ml] for the salad)
- [ ] 1½ tbsp (22 ml) chili garlic sauce or sriracha (1 tbsp [15 ml] for the fried rice, ½ tbsp [7 ml] for the salads)
- [ ] 2 tbsp (30 ml) sesame oil (4 tsp [20 ml] for the salads, the rest for the fried rice)
- [ ] 3 tbsp (45 ml) olive oil (1 tbsp [15 ml] per meal)
- [ ] Cooking spray
- [ ] ⅓ cup (80 g) peanut or nut butter of your choice
- [ ] 3 tbsp (45 ml) agave or honey, plus more to taste

- [ ] 3 tbsp (45 ml) rice vinegar
- [ ] 1 tbsp (15 ml) vegetable oil
- [ ] 1 cup (146 g) peanuts, crushed
- [ ] ¾ cup (150 g) rice
- [ ] 2 tsp (10 ml) sriracha, optional
- [ ] 1 tsp sugar
- [ ] 1 (15-oz [420-ml]) can tomato sauce
- [ ] 1 (15-oz [420-ml]) can fire-roasted diced tomatoes
- [ ] 1 (15-oz [420-ml]) can pinto beans
- [ ] 2 cups (300 g) of macaroni elbows
- [ ] 2 cups (480 ml) vegetable broth

FRIDGE

- [ ] 1 (14-oz [392-ml]) package of firm tofu
- [ ] 5 eggs
- [ ] 1 cup (170 g) kimchi, chopped and 2 tbsp (30 ml) kimchi liquid from the jar
- [ ] 1 cup (136 g) canned or frozen corn, thawed
- [ ] 1¼ cups (120 g) shredded cheddar cheese

SPICES

- [ ] Salt and pepper
- [ ] 1 tsp cumin
- [ ] 1½ tsp (3 g) chili powder

Omnivore 5-day Workweek Meal Plan

Lunch	Mission-Style Steak Burrito Bowls (page 65) with Creamy Avocado Herb Sauce (page 160)	Jerk Shrimp, Corn & Black Bean Salad (page 86) with Creamy Avocado Herb Sauce (page 160)	Jerk Shrimp, Corn & Black Bean Salad (page 86) with Creamy Avocado Herb Sauce (page 160)	Cozy Chicken Tortilla Soup (page 115)	Cozy Chicken Tortilla Soup (page 115)
Dinner	Jerk Shrimp, Corn & Black Bean Salad (page 86) with Creamy Avocado Herb Sauce (page 160)	Mission-Style Steak Burrito Bowls (page 65) with Creamy Avocado Herb Sauce (page 160)	Mission-Style Steak Burrito Bowls (page 65) with Creamy Avocado Herb Sauce (page 160)	OPEN	OPEN

TIPS

- Make the avocado herb sauce for the salads and the burrito bowls.

- Any leftover beans from the salad or bowls can go in the soup.

- You'll have four total servings of the tortilla soup. Store them all in the freezer, enjoy two for this week's plan and save the remaining two for another busy week!

- On prep day, first marinate the steak for the burrito bowls, and then make the shrimp salad. Get the tortilla soup started as you finish the burrito bowls.

- The pickled onions go with the Jerk Shrimp, Corn & Black Bean Salad (page 86) and can be used as a topping for the Mission-Style Steak Burrito Bowls (page 65)

Grocery List

Pink = Mission-Style Steak Burrito Bowls (page 65)

Blue = Jerk Shrimp, Corn & Black Bean Salad (page 86)

Green = Cozy Chicken Tortilla Soup (page 115)

Orange = Creamy Avocado Herb Sauce (page 160)

Purple = Quick Pickled Red Onions (page 168)

Black = Overlapping Ingredients

PRODUCE

- [ ] 4 limes (2 for the bowls, 1 for the salads, 1 for the soup)
- [ ] 3 lemons
- [ ] 7 cloves garlic (divided among all the recipes)
- [ ] 3 avocados (1 for the bowls, 1 for the avocado sauce, 1 for the soup)
- [ ] 6 scallions (3 for the soup, 3 for the salads)
- [ ] ½ cup (120 ml) orange or grapefruit juice
- [ ] 1 bunch cilantro
- [ ] 1 red bell pepper
- [ ] 4 radishes
- [ ] 1 (9-oz [255-g]) bag of lettuce or romaine (about 8 cups)
- [ ] 1 cup (160 g) chopped yellow onion
- [ ] 1 red bell pepper, chopped
- [ ] 1 medium red onion, sliced thin
- [ ] 2 cups (32 g) of fresh mixed herb leaves (basil, cilantro, parsley, mint, dill, etc.)

PANTRY

- [ ] ⅔ cup (160 ml) olive oil (divided among all the recipes)
- [ ] ½ cup (120 ml) vegetable oil (for cooking the steak in the bowl meals and shrimp in the salads)
- [ ] 2 tsp (10 ml) honey or white sugar
- [ ] ¾ cup (50 g) white rice
- [ ] ½ cup (90 g) salsa
- [ ] 2 (15-oz [420-ml]) cans of pinto beans
- [ ] 1 tsp sugar
- [ ] 1 cup (136 g) canned or frozen corn, thawed
- [ ] 1 cup (172 g) black beans, rinsed and drained
- [ ] 2–3 chipotle peppers in adobo sauce

- [ ] 2 tsp (10 ml) adobo sauce (from can of peppers)
- [ ] 1 (28-oz [784-ml]) can crushed tomatoes
- [ ] 1 (14-oz [392-ml]) can cream style corn
- [ ] 2 cups (480 ml) chicken broth
- [ ] Tortilla chips of your choice
- [ ] ½ cup (120 ml) apple cider vinegar
- [ ] ¼ cup (50 g) sugar

FRIDGE

- [ ] 1 lb (454 g) flank steak, cut into 2 big pieces
- [ ] Sour cream
- [ ] Pico de gallo
- [ ] 1 lb (454 g) shrimp, peeled and deveined
- [ ] 12 oz (336 g) chicken breast, cut in half if thick
- [ ] 1 cup (113 g) of shredded cheese
- [ ] 2 tbsp (30 ml) plain yogurt, sour cream or tahini

SPICES

- [ ] Salt and pepper
- [ ] 4 ½ tsp (9 g) cumin (1½ tsp [3 g] for the bowls, 3 tsp [6 g] for the soup)
- [ ] 2 ½ tsp (6 g) chili powder (½ tsp for the bowls, 2 tsp [4 g] for the soup)
- [ ] ¾ tsp cayenne (¼ tsp per meal)
- [ ] 1 tsp garlic powder
- [ ] ½ tsp paprika
- [ ] ½ tsp ground thyme
- [ ] ½ tsp allspice
- [ ] ½ tsp cinnamon
- [ ] 1 tsp dried oregano
- [ ] ¼ tsp crushed red pepper, optional

Flexitarian 5-Day Workweek Meal Plan

Lunch	Salmon & Sweet Potato Sheet Pan (page 36)	Black Bean, Spinach & Pesto Quesadillas (page 138)	Salmon & Sweet Potato Sheet Pan (page 36)	Cheesy Penne Spinach Pesto Bake (page 123)	Cheesy Penne Spinach Pesto Bake (page 123)
Dinner	Black Bean, Spinach & Pesto Quesadillas (page 138)	Salmon & Sweet Potato Sheet Pan (page 36)	Black Bean, Spinach & Pesto Quesadillas (page 138)	OPEN	OPEN

TIPS

- You'll have four total servings of the pasta bake. Store them all in the freezer, enjoy two for this week's plan and save the remaining two for another busy week!

- On prep day, first chop everything you need for all three meals. Then, get the sheet-pan salmon in the oven while you cook the filling for the quesadillas. Set the filling aside and assemble the pasta bake. Finish the quesadillas while the pasta bakes in the oven.

Grocery List

Pink = Salmon & Sweet Potato Sheet Pan (page 36)

Blue = Black Bean, Spinach & Pesto Quesadillas (page 138)

Green = Cheesy Penne Spinach Pesto Bake (page 123)

Black = Overlapping Ingredients

PRODUCE

- [ ] 3 cloves garlic (1 for the sheet pan meal, 2 for the pasta bake)
- [ ] 1 lb (454 g) sweet potatoes
- [ ] 12 oz (336 g) green beans
- [ ] ½ cup (80 g) chopped yellow onion (about ½ an onion)
- [ ] 3 cups (100 g) spinach
- [ ] 2 cups (298 g) cherry tomatoes
- [ ] 1 head broccoli
- [ ] 1½ cups (42 g) basil
- [ ] 2 tbsp (30 ml) lemon juice

PANTRY

- [ ] 1 cup (240 ml) olive oil (divided among all the recipes)
- [ ] Cooking spray (for all the recipes)
- [ ] 1 tbsp (15 ml) honey or agave
- [ ] 3 tbsp (45 ml) soy sauce
- [ ] 1 (15-oz [420-ml]) can black beans, rinsed and drained
- [ ] ⅔ cup (96 g) pesto
- [ ] ½ cup (90 g) kalamata olives
- [ ] 2 cups (108 g) sun-dried tomatoes
- [ ] 3 large 10-inch (25-cm) tortillas
- [ ] 8 oz (226 lb) penne
- [ ] ½ cup (54 g) almonds or walnuts

FRIDGE

- [ ] 1 lb (454 g) salmon
- [ ] 1 cup (150 g) crumbled feta cheese
- [ ] 2 (8-oz [226-g]) bags shredded mozzarella
- [ ] 3 chicken sausage links
- [ ] ½ cup (50 g) grated Parmesan cheese

SPICES

- [ ] Salt and pepper
- [ ] ¼ tsp cinnamon
- [ ] ½ tsp cumin
- [ ] 1 tsp oregano

Pescatarian 5-Day Workweek Meal Plan

Lunch	Moroccan-Inspired Salmon Couscous Bowls (page 76) with All-Purpose Tahini Lemon Sauce (page 163)	Green Tuna Pasta Salad (page 58)	Moroccan-Inspired Salmon Couscous Bowls (page 76) with All-Purpose Tahini Lemon Sauce (page 163)	White Bean Chili Verde (page 116)	White Bean Chili Verde (page 116)
Dinner	Green Tuna Pasta Salad (page 58)	Moroccan-Inspired Salmon Couscous Bowls (page 76) with All-Purpose Tahini Lemon Sauce (page 163)	Green Tuna Pasta Salad (page 58)	OPEN	OPEN

TIPS

- You'll have four total servings of the green chili. Store them all in the freezer, enjoy two for this week's plan and save the remaining two for another busy week!

- Any leftover vegetables from the burgers or pasta can be added to the chili.

- On prep day, chop everything you need for each meal. Get the Moroccan salmon recipe in the oven, then start the chili verde. While it simmers, cook the tuna pasta meal.

Grocery List

Pink = Moroccan-Inspired Salmon Couscous Bowls (page 76)

Blue = Green Tuna Pasta Salad (page 58)

Green = White Bean Chili Verde (page 116)

Purple = All-Purpose Tahini Lemon Sauce (page 163)

Black = Overlapping Ingredients

PRODUCE

- [ ] 1 yellow onion (½ for the chili, ½ for the salmon bowl)
- [ ] 7 cloves garlic, minced (divided among all recipes)
- [ ] 1½ cups (90 g) chopped parsley, optional (1 cup [60 g] for the salmon bowls, the rest for the tuna pasta)
- [ ] 3 lemons (for the salmon bowls and the tuna pasta)
- [ ] 1 bunch cilantro (½ for the tuna pasta, ½ for the chili verde)
- [ ] 2 avocados (1 for the tuna pasta, 1 for the chili verde)
- [ ] 1 medium eggplant
- [ ] 1 small cauliflower
- [ ] 2 carrots
- [ ] 12 oz (336 g) asparagus
- [ ] ½ cup (15 g) basil
- [ ] ½ cup (80 g) chopped red onion (sub shallots)
- [ ] 1 poblano pepper, chopped
- [ ] 1 jalapeño, seeded and chopped
- [ ] 3 scallions

PANTRY

- [ ] 6 tbsp (90 ml) olive oil (divided among all the recipes)
- [ ] ⅔ cup (113 g) couscous
- [ ] 1 tbsp (15 ml) honey
- [ ] 6 oz (170 g) bowtie pasta (about 2 cups)
- [ ] 1 tbsp (15 ml) Dijon mustard
- [ ] 2 (5-oz [142-ml]) cans of tuna packed in oil

- [ ] ⅓ cup (18 g) sun-dried tomatoes
- [ ] 2 (15-oz [420-ml]) cans of white beans
- [ ] 1 (15-oz [420-ml]) can enchilada sauce
- [ ] 1 (10-oz [283-ml]) can Rotel
- [ ] Tortilla chips, optional for serving
- [ ] ⅓ cup (80 ml) tahini

FRIDGE

- [ ] 1 lb (454 g) salmon, cut into 3 pieces
- [ ] ⅓ cup (80 ml) plain Greek yogurt
- [ ] 2 tbsp (30 ml) sour cream, plus extra for topping, optional
- [ ] Shredded cheese, optional for serving

SPICES

- [ ] Salt and pepper
- [ ] 1½ tsp (4 g) cumin
- [ ] ½ tsp turmeric
- [ ] ½ tsp paprika
- [ ] ¼ tsp allspice
- [ ] ¼ tsp cinnamon
- [ ] 1 tsp chili powder
- [ ] ½ tsp chipotle powder

The Prepper's Pantry

Here's a list of items you'll want to keep in your kitchen to make meal prepping lunches from this cookbook easier.

PANTRY

- [ ] Cooking spray
- [ ] Olive oil
- [ ] Vegetable oil
- [ ] Pasta: short pasta (orzo, shells) and spaghetti
- [ ] Rice noodles and/or ramen noodles
- [ ] Grains: rice, quinoa, farro
- [ ] Pinto beans
- [ ] Black beans
- [ ] Refried beans
- [ ] Chickpeas
- [ ] Coconut milk
- [ ] Canned diced tomatoes
- [ ] Chicken and/or vegetable stock
- [ ] Red wine vinegar
- [ ] Apple cider vinegar
- [ ] Canned chipotles in adobo sauce
- [ ] Honey, agave or maple syrup
- [ ] Soy sauce
- [ ] Sesame oil
- [ ] Nut butter of your choice
- [ ] Breadcrumbs: panko or traditional
- [ ] White sugar
- [ ] Brown sugar
- [ ] Vanilla extract
- [ ] All-purpose flour or gluten-free flour

- [ ] Tortilla chips
- [ ] Tuna packed in oil (for omnivores)
- [ ] Nuts: peanuts, walnuts, pepitas
- [ ] Brown lentils
- [ ] Tomato paste
- [ ] Sun-dried tomatoes

FREEZER

- [ ] Chicken breast and/or thighs (for omnivores)
- [ ] Steak (for omnivores)
- [ ] Ground meat (for omnivores)
- [ ] Shrimp (for pescatarians)
- [ ] Salmon (for pescatarians)
- [ ] Chicken sausage (for omnivores)
- [ ] Chorizo (for omnivores)
- [ ] Pizza dough
- [ ] Frozen peas
- [ ] Frozen corn
- [ ] Sandwich bread

FRIDGE

- [ ] Ketchup
- [ ] Salsa
- [ ] Butter
- [ ] Tahini
- [ ] Lemons and limes
- [ ] Rice vinegar
- [ ] Sriracha or chili garlic sauce
- [ ] Worcestershire sauce
- [ ] Dijon mustard
- [ ] Mayonnaise

- [ ] Sour cream
- [ ] Tortillas: large for wraps and small
- [ ] Cheese: feta, shredded cheddar, shredded mozzarella
- [ ] Firm tofu (for vegans/vegetarians/flexitarians)
- [ ] Marinara
- [ ] Kalamata olives
- [ ] Kimchi
- [ ] Pesto
- [ ] Red curry paste
- [ ] Hot sauce

SPICES

- [ ] Sesame seeds
- [ ] Furikake seasoning
- [ ] Kosher salt
- [ ] Ground pepper
- [ ] Cumin
- [ ] Turmeric
- [ ] Paprika
- [ ] Allspice
- [ ] Cinnamon
- [ ] Chili powder
- [ ] Chipotle powder
- [ ] Garlic powder
- [ ] Crushed red pepper
- [ ] Ground thyme
- [ ] Dried oregano
- [ ] Curry powder
- [ ] Garam masala
- [ ] Dried parsley
- [ ] Taco seasoning

Pantry Tips & Swap Notes

RICE

Whenever you see rice listed in a recipe, know it was tested with white rice. If you use brown rice, cooking times will be a bit longer. I do not recommend making any rice skillets or bakes with brown rice, but it can be used as a swap for any recipe where rice is used on the side.

GLUTEN-FREE SWAPS

Soy sauce: tamari or liquid aminos

Pasta: gluten-free pasta of your choice

Pizza dough: gluten-free dough of your choice

Farro: quinoa, rice or gluten-free grain of your choice

Tortillas: gluten-free tortillas of your choice (Note that gluten-free tortillas don't hold together as well and it's best to not pre-roll wrap meals with gluten-free tortillas.)

VEGAN/VEGETARIAN SWAPS

Animal protein: All animal proteins in this book can be swapped for tofu, tempeh, veggie "meat" and veggie burgers. Lentils, edamame, chickpeas and black beans can be used in soups, stews and curries that include meat.

Honey: You can use pure maple syrup or agave for any dish containing honey.

Milk: Use any plant-based milk of your choice for recipes containing milk.

Kimchi: You can generally find vegan kimchi in grocery stores that carry kimchi.

Worcestershire sauce: Soy sauce

Shredded cheese: Dairy-free cheese of your choice

Parmesan cheese: Nutritional yeast is generally the best swap for Parmesan cheese.

Meat broth/stock: Vegetable broth or water will always work.

Eggs: In this book, eggs can be left out for vegans.

Mayonnaise: Vegan mayonnaise or tahini always does the trick!

Sour cream: We use sour cream as a topping for various meal prep recipes in this book! Plain vegan yogurt or cashew cream would work well as a substitute.

OTHER ALLERGENS

If you're allergic to nuts, leave them out in these recipes.

If you don't eat soy, replace tofu with proteins you like and see above for soy sauce swaps.

If avoiding nightshades, swap those vegetables out for ones you do eat! Vegetables are the easiest items to swap in any recipe.

Can't eat onions or garlic? Skip them in these recipes.

MAKE YOUR MEALS LAST

Choosing the Right Containers

Whether you're new to meal prep or you're a seasoned pro, the containers you have for meal prep could mean the difference between loving and hating your meals.

The general size for meal prep containers for the lunch/dinner recipes in this book are 30-ounce (887-ml) containers that hold about 3 cups of food.

No matter what kind of containers you get, make sure they have snap lids. Containers with snap lids are much less likely to leak!

If you've never meal prepped before, pick up a cheap three- or four-pack of 30-ounce (887-ml) plastic containers (or anything around that size) before investing in high quality glass containers. It's the best low-cost way to figure out what size works best for you.

If you commute via public transportation, walk or bike to work every day, get quality BPA-free plastic containers. Plastic containers are great for commuting because they're light to carry with you and easy to wash at work. There's nothing unsafe about microwaving BPA-free plastic as long as you don't see any scratches in the containers. Once they get a bit scratched up, it's time to retire them from food and use them for storing other items in your house. Plastic containers are freezer safe, but you can't reheat them in the oven!

If you work from home or drive to work, grab glass containers with sturdy snap lids. Glass containers are my favorite for meal prep because they last

the longest, are easiest to clean (they don't stain) and there's something about eating out of a glass container that makes meal prep feel a bit fancier.

For glass containers, you want to look for ones that are oven safe. That way you know you can reheat your meals in the oven if you'd like. Not all glass containers are automatically oven safe.

Containers with dividers are great for stir-fries and any meal with rice on the side. I use them mostly for curries, like our Lentil Butternut Squash Coconut Curry (page 124), and meals where the elements need to be heated separately.

Stainless steel lunchboxes are fantastic for cold snack lunches like our Soft-Boiled Egg & Smoked Salmon Snack Lunchbox (page 50) but cannot be reheated in the microwave.

For dressings, I love the small plastic containers with lids that you can usually find in the grocery store. They're affordable, easy to clean and can easily be tucked into a larger container.

If you don't have a ton of fridge space, I recommend using large containers to store entire meals in, rather than portioning meals into individual containers.

Storage and Reheating Tips & Tricks

STORING MEALS

The most common question I get about meal prep is: *How do you store the meals and for how long?*

The general rule of thumb is that any prepared meal is good in the fridge for 4 days, not counting the day you cooked it. So, if you made a meal on Sunday, you ideally want to eat it by Thursday.

However, this rule is based more on our mindset around leftovers than anything else. Technically speaking, if a meal is cooked properly and safely and your fridge is at the right temperature—40°F (4.5°C)—and doesn't lose power, a meal can be safe to consume for 7 days after cooking. But! No one really wants to eat food they know is 7 days old, so that's why I recommend aiming to eat your meal preps within 4 to 5 days max.

All meals are meant to be stored in airtight containers in the fridge or in the freezer. Again, it is super important to have lids that snap tightly onto the containers. A big no-no is storing meals in a dish or on a plate wrapped in saran wrap. That can work for about a day, but after a few days the meal won't be nearly as fresh as it would be in a regular container.

The meals in this cookbook were specifically made to taste great for meal prep, because not all meals are made to be tasty as leftovers!

Here are some tips to keep your meals tasting and feeling fresh all week long.

1. Let meals cool down before you cover them and store them in the fridge. If you cover meals right after cooking, condensation will collect inside your container which will make your food soggy. It's safer to let meals cool to room temperature before storing! Make sure to store them within 2 to 3 hours of cooking.

2. Always keep sauces and dressings on the side until you eat the meal. Pouring a dressing on a salad a day before you eat it will leave you with a very soggy meal!

3. Garnishes go a long way with meal prep. You'll find a handful of sliced scallions or a lemon wedge in your container makes it feel less like leftovers. This is part of the intentionality that makes the difference between leftover food and meal prepped food.

REHEATING MEALS

How you reheat meals can also affect the outcome! When in doubt, for any meal that should be eaten warm, the microwave on medium power is a solid option, especially when reheating meat. But if you don't have a microwave, you should reheat meals where you cooked them. If you baked or roasted a meal, reheat it in the oven. If it was cooked in a pan on the stove, reheat it on the stove.

Know that all foods are safe to reheat in any appliance as long as they were cooked properly through the first time, especially meat. Reheated food is safe to eat as long as it warms up to around 150°F (65°C).

When reheating rice or pasta, partially cover the meal prep container so that the rice or pasta can steam. This helps avoid that hard, crunchy texture. Or, you can add a few drops of water to the container to get moisture back into the rice or pasta.

When reheating wraps or anything with a tortilla, wrap it in a dry paper towel when reheating in the microwave. This soaks up extra moisture and keeps your tortilla dry. It's also ideal to reheat tortilla meals on the stove, in the oven or toaster oven or in an air fryer to crisp them up, if you can!

If you're taking meals on the go and don't have fridge access, meals are okay for about 3 to 4 hours out of the fridge in mild weather. But don't leave food in a hot car or in a warm spot for that long!

What to Do When You're Not In the Mood

As I mentioned earlier, life happens. And sometimes, you're just not going to want what you meal prepped. That's totally normal and is nothing to feel guilty about! Sometimes, we just can't predict what we'll want, and every week is a chance to get better. I've been meal prepping for several years and am still learning new ways to improve my own personal system.

When you're not in the mood to eat what you meal prepped, you have a few options other than tossing or composting the meal.

1. You can save the meal for the following day. This is why we don't prep every meal and lock ourselves into eating a bunch of food we might not want.

2. Depending on the meal, you can freeze it. Future you will be so thankful!

3. You can give it to a friend, family member or coworker.

4. You can repurpose it into something else—see below!

TIPS FOR REPURPOSING MEAL PREPS

Not in the mood for that lunch on day three? Transform it into something new! Here are some easy ideas for repurposing meal preps. You'll notice that quite a few of these involve tortillas, which are the real MVP of transforming meals into something new because they're so versatile and last weeks in the fridge.

- Turn salads like the Jerk Shrimp, Corn & Black Bean Salad (page 86) into tacos, nachos, sandwiches, wraps or quesadillas.

- Toss roasted veggies from the Sheet Pan Roasted Vegetables (page 152) with pasta and sauce.

- Add prepped veggies from a recipe like My Favorite Spinach Greek Salad (page 93) to a quick egg scramble or frittata.

- Chop prepped chicken, fish, shrimp, steak or tofu from one meal and add it into a salad.

- Turn leftover chili from the White Bean Chili Verde (page 116) into nachos or toss with pasta and cheese for an easy chili mac.

- Use prepped veggies from Moroccan-Inspired Salmon Couscous Bowls (page 76) in ramen, soups, chilis or stews.

- Leftover rice from meals like the Mango Tofu & Coconut Rice Bowls (page 75) and My Go-To Teriyaki Chicken & Veggies (page 102) is perfect for fried rice meals!

- Transform leftovers from dishes like the Chorizo Sweet Potato Black Bean Skillet (page 39) into a stuffed pepper or squash meal.

- Use your meal preps for pizza toppings! The ingredients from the Buffalo Chicken Tacos (page 141) would be delicious on a pizza, with ranch of course.

It can be pretty fun to deconstruct your meal prepped lunches and turn them into something else instead of wasting them. I hope you come back to this list anytime you're out of ideas of what to do with meals that you're not in the mood for.

LOW-MAINTENANCE MEALS

Sometimes, life happens and we don't have much time and energy to cook lunches ahead of time. Enter: Low-maintenance meal preps. These are the meals you'll go to when you're feeling low energy and don't want to do a pile of dishes.

If you're all about that one-pot life, we've included recipes like the Mushroom & Parmesan Orzo Skillet (page 35), which was inspired by risotto and can be made all in one pan. Most of these recipes take less than 45 minutes to make as well, so you'll only be in the kitchen for about an hour, including cleaning up. It's always worth it when you don't have to worry about food for lunches during the week, thanks to that hour you spent prepping a meal over the weekend!

Some of these meals require two pots, but they're still super easy. The Swiss Chard & Ground Beef Pasta Skillet (page 32) is a favorite from the Workweek Lunch Meal Prep Program. You boil the pasta in one pot and cook the veggies and sauce in another pan or pot. The same goes for the Sheet Pan Veggie Pizza (page 40), which requires rice on the side, but everything else is cooked in one skillet.

This chapter also includes a meal I've prepped for lunch since day one: the Salmon & Sweet Potato Sheet Pan (page 36). I could eat this meal every day. Once you get everything on the sheet pan, you can clean up while it bakes and then you're done.

Most of these meals reheat well in the microwave or on the stove. These easy meals are proof that meal prep doesn't always have to be a big project!

Swiss Chard & Ground Beef Pasta Skillet

Sometimes, the simple meals are the ones we look forward to most. This humble pasta dish reheats so well, it has become a staple in my home, and we always look forward to it for work lunches. It has the coziness of a Bolognese, but without all the hard work. It feels so good to use up a lot of Swiss chard in this recipe, but it works well with spinach and kale too! And if you want to use ground turkey or veggie ground "meat" instead of ground beef, that totally works as well.

Prep Time: 5 minutes | Cook Time: 25 minutes | Servings: 3

2½ cups (170 g) small pasta shells

1 tbsp (15 ml) olive oil

1 lb (454 g) ground beef

2 cloves garlic, minced

½ tsp salt, plus more to taste

¼ tsp ground pepper, plus more to taste

1 (28-oz [784-ml]) can crushed tomatoes

½ tsp oregano

½ tsp dried basil or parsley

⅔ cup (160 ml) heavy cream

2 cups (134 g) chopped Swiss chard or kale (about ½ a bunch)

½ cup (50 g) grated Parmesan cheese, plus more for serving

Bring a pot of water to boil and cook the pasta according to the package—generally around 10 minutes for shells. If the pasta is done before you're ready to use it, drain the water from the pot and keep the pasta covered.

Add the olive oil to a skillet over medium heat, followed by the ground beef, garlic, salt and pepper. Brown the beef by stirring it frequently for 7 to 10 minutes, until it's no longer pink.

Add the entire can of crushed tomatoes, oregano and dried basil and more salt and pepper to taste. Bring the mixture to a low boil and cook for about 5 more minutes over medium heat. Then pour the heavy cream into the tomato-beef mixture. Stir to combine. Taste the mixture and adjust the seasonings as needed. Let the mixture cook for about 10 minutes to let the flavors mix and the sauce thicken slightly.

Turn off the heat. Add in the cooked pasta and chopped Swiss chard. Stir until the greens wilt and the pasta is covered in sauce. Finally, stir in the Parmesan cheese. Add more salt if desired.

Divide the mixture among three or four meal prep containers. Add more Parmesan cheese on top if desired.

Storage, Reheating and Serving Notes: This pasta skillet can last in the fridge for up to 5 days. It's freezer friendly for up to 6 months. You can reheat this meal in the microwave or on the stove. Add a splash of water to the container while reheating if the pasta is very stuck together.

Mushroom & Parmesan Orzo Skillet

We might disagree here, but I don't think risotto is meal prep friendly because the next day it's more stodgy than creamy, not to mention all that stirring in making it! But this mushroom orzo skillet IS! And it was inspired by the flavors you often see in a traditional risotto. Orzo is a truly underrated pasta that we love for meal prep. It cooks quickly, reheats better than other pastas and is fun to eat. But if needed, ditalini or another small pasta works. When in doubt, cook your favorite pasta on the side and add it to the skillet ingredients toward the end of cooking. To make this meal vegetarian, I recommend using veggie sausage links.

Prep Time: 10 minutes | Cook Time: 30 minutes | Servings: 3

1 tbsp (15 ml) olive oil

3 Italian chicken sausage links, sliced

8 oz (226 g) baby bella mushrooms, sliced

1 cup (112 g) orzo

3 cloves garlic, minced

½ tsp thyme

1½ cups (360 ml) chicken stock or water, plus more as needed if the pasta sticks

½ tsp salt

¼ tsp ground pepper

⅓ cup (80 ml) milk (I use 2%)

2 tbsp (28 g) butter

½ cup (50 g) grated Parmesan cheese, plus more for serving

4 oz (113 g) spinach, chopped

Heat up a large skillet over medium heat for a minute or two, then add the olive oil. After a minute or two, add the chicken sausage slices and let them cook for about 5 minutes, stirring occasionally. Add the mushrooms and cook for 5 more minutes, until the mushrooms start to become fragrant.

Add the orzo, garlic, thyme and chicken stock with the salt and pepper. Stir, bring the mixture to a boil and then cover and cook on low heat for 10 to 12 minutes, until the orzo is cooked through. If the orzo sticks to the bottom of the pan or looks very dry, use a spatula to scrape up any orzo off the pan and add a little more broth or water.

When the orzo is cooked through, stir in the milk, butter and Parmesan cheese. Turn off the heat and stir in the spinach. Cover the pan to let the spinach wilt.

Divide the mushroom orzo among three meal prep containers. Top with extra Parmesan cheese.

Storage, Reheating and Serving Notes: This orzo skillet can last in the fridge for up to 4 days. It's not freezer friendly. I recommend reheating it with a splash of water in the microwave or on the stove. The water helps the pasta break up a bit.

Salmon & Sweet Potato Sheet Pan

Can you believe salmon is the first meal I learned to meal prep successfully? Salmon is often intimidating to the novice cook, but baking it with a soy and honey glaze is foolproof. The salmon, green veggie and sweet potato combo is something I've seen frequently at fast-casual lunch spots, and I quickly found out that making it at home is not only easy, but much more budget friendly. You can make this over and over by switching the green beans out for different veggies and salmon for different proteins.

Prep Time: 10 minutes | Cook Time: 30 minutes | Servings: 3

FOR THE VEGGIES

1 lb (454 g) sweet potatoes, chopped into big chunks

¼ tsp cinnamon

½ tsp cumin

1 tsp salt, divided

½ tsp pepper, divided

2 tbsp (30 ml) olive oil, divided

12 oz (336 g) green beans, ends trimmed

FOR THE SALMON

1 tbsp (15 ml) honey

3 tbsp (45 ml) soy sauce

1 clove garlic, minced

1 tbsp (15 ml) olive oil

1 lb (454 g) salmon, cut into 3 pieces

½ tsp salt

¼ tsp ground pepper

Preheat your oven to 425°F (220°C).

To a bowl, add the sweet potatoes, cinnamon, cumin, half of the salt and pepper and 1 tablespoon (15 ml) of olive oil. Mix well and pour onto a baking sheet. Place in the oven and bake for 25 to 30 minutes, flipping halfway through, until the sweet potatoes are soft and darker in color.

Add the green beans to the same bowl with the remaining olive oil, salt and pepper. Toss well, and then pour onto a second baking sheet. Place the green beans in a way that leaves room in the center of the sheet pan for the salmon!

In a measuring glass, mix the honey, soy sauce and garlic. Pour 1 tablespoon (15 ml) of olive oil in the center of the baking sheet and spread it around a bit—this is where the salmon will go. Place the salmon skin side down on the sheet pan. Add salt and pepper to the salmon, then spoon the soy-honey mixture on top. Use a spoon or brush to spread it all over the salmon. Bake for 15 to 20 minutes, until the salmon is firm to the touch and the green beans are cooked through.

Divide the sweet potato, green beans and salmon among three meal prep containers.

Storage, Reheating and Serving Notes: This meal can last in the fridge for 3 to 4 days. It's not freezer friendly. You can reheat it in the oven, stove or microwave. If using the microwave, I recommend lower power for salmon, if you can.

Chorizo Sweet Potato Black Bean Skillet

This is not your typical rice and beans dish! Rice skillets can be a little tricky to get used to cooking. If you're new to this kind of meal, I recommend cooking the rice on the side and then adding it to the skillet ingredients at the end of cooking. Using white rice is recommended here, since it cooks much faster than brown rice. Making this meal without meat is easy if you can find "soyrizo," or soy chorizo. This skillet meal would also make a great filling for burritos, tacos or piled on nachos.

Prep Time: 10 minutes | Cook Time: 30 minutes | Servings: 3

2 tbsp (30 ml) olive oil, divided

½ cup (80 g) chopped yellow onion (about ½ an onion)

1 tsp salt, divided

1½ cups (210 g) chopped sweet potato (about ½ a large sweet potato)

½ tsp chili powder

½ tsp cumin

¼ tsp ground pepper

8 oz (226 g) chorizo (sub ground meat of your choice)

1 (15-oz [420-ml]) can black beans, rinsed and drained

½ cup (100 g) white rice

½ cup (90 g) salsa

⅔ cup (160 ml) water

½ cup (12 g) cilantro, packed, plus more for garnish

½ cup (57 g) shredded cheddar cheese

Heat a large skillet over medium heat for a few minutes, then add half of the olive oil. After a minute, add the onion and ¼ teaspoon of salt. Cook over medium heat, stirring often until the onion is translucent and fragrant, about 5 minutes.

Add the sweet potato, chili powder, cumin, pepper and another ¼ teaspoon of salt to the pan. If the pan looks dry, add a splash of water. Toss the sweet potato to coat it in the spices, and then cover the pan and let it cook over medium heat for about 10 minutes, stirring occasionally.

When the potatoes have softened slightly, push them to the sides of the pan. Add the remaining oil, followed by the chorizo. Break up the chorizo with a spatula or wooden spoon as it cooks over medium heat. Continue to stir and cook the chorizo until it's fully cooked through and brown.

Add the black beans, rice, salsa, water and remaining salt. Stir well. Bring the mixture to a boil, then cover and continue to cook over low heat for about 15 minutes, or until the rice is soft and fully cooked. Then turn the heat off and stir in the cilantro.

Divide the skillet among three meal prep containers. Top with cheese and extra cilantro.

Storage, Reheating and Serving Notes: This meal can last in the fridge for up to 5 days. It's freezer friendly for up to 6 months. You can reheat it in the microwave or on the stove!

Sheet Pan Veggie Pizza

Yes, you can meal prep pizza for work! Pizza works so well for work lunches if you're working from home, have access to a toaster oven at work or if you love eating pizza cold. Personally, if I have oven access, I'm heating it up. When in doubt, use the microwave or the stove. This veggie pizza involves my all-time favorite combination of ingredients. Sweet tomatoes, crunchy bell peppers, umami mushrooms and savory olives between layers of melty mozzarella cheese is a huge upgrade to your standard office pizza lunch.

Prep Time: 10 minutes | Cook Time: 30 minutes | Servings: 3

Cooking spray, optional

2 tbsp (30 ml) olive oil, divided

1 cup (113 g) sliced baby bella mushrooms

½ tsp salt

¼ tsp ground pepper

⅓ cup (41 g) all-purpose flour

1 lb (425 g) pizza dough (I use store bought)

1½ cups (360 ml) marinara sauce

2 cups (226 g) shredded mozzarella cheese

1 small Roma tomato, sliced

1 medium green bell pepper, chopped

½ cup (90 g) kalamata olives, chopped

⅓ cup (53 g) sliced red onion

½ cup (50 g) grated Parmesan cheese

Preheat your oven to 450°F (232°C). Prepare a sheet pan with cooking spray, parchment paper or a Silpat mat.

Heat up half of the olive oil in a skillet over medium heat. Add the mushrooms with the salt and pepper. Let the mushrooms cook for 7 to 8 minutes, stirring occasionally, until they've softened and reduced in size. Turn off the heat.

On a flat, clean surface, spread out the flour a bit. Dust your hands with some as well. Lay the pizza dough out and roll it with a rolling pin into the shape of your sheet pan, a big rectangle. Then carefully place it on the sheet pan and stretch it to the edges of the pan as needed.

Spread the remaining tablespoon of olive oil over the dough, then spread a layer of the marinara on the dough, leaving a clean edge for the crust.

Sprinkle half of the mozzarella cheese in an even layer over the sauce. Then place the mushrooms, tomato slices, bell pepper, olives and sliced red onion evenly all over the cheese layer. Add the remaining mozzarella cheese and sprinkle the Parmesan cheese on top. Bake for 15 to 20 minutes, until the crust is golden and the cheese has completely melted.

Let the pizza cool completely before slicing into six pieces. You can store two pieces in one container or wrapped in foil together, separated by a layer of parchment paper. Repeat with the remaining slices.

Storage, Reheating and Serving Notes: This pizza will last in the fridge for up to 4 days and can be frozen for up to 6 months. I recommend reheating it in the oven, toaster oven or in a pan on the stove. The microwave can work, too, but it won't be crispy!

Broccoli Cheddar Soup

This humble one-pot soup hits the spot between meetings and calls at work! Instead of using heavy cream or half and half, which is traditional for this recipe, we're using regular milk without sacrificing any of the thickness, thanks to the roux made in the second step of this recipe. If you don't like broccoli, this would work well with cauliflower too. This recipe is not freezer friendly, so make sure to whip it up on a week where you'll need a cozy meal to get you through.

Prep Time: 10 minutes | Cook Time: 30 minutes | Servings: 4

2 tbsp (30 ml) olive oil or butter

½ cup (80 g) chopped yellow onion (about ½ an onion)

2 cloves garlic, minced

¼ cup (31 g) all-purpose flour or gluten-free flour

1 tsp salt, plus more to taste

½ tsp ground pepper, plus more to taste

1 tsp paprika

1 tsp ground mustard

2 cups (480 ml) chicken or vegetable stock

3 cups (273 g) broccoli florets, chopped

2 carrots, chopped

2 cups (480 ml) milk (I used 2%)

2 cups (224 g) shredded cheddar cheese, plus more for topping

¼ tsp cayenne, optional

Crusty bread, for serving

Warm up a large Dutch oven or stock pot over medium heat for a few minutes, then add the olive oil. After a minute, add the onion and sauté, stirring often, for 4 to 5 minutes, until the onion is soft and fragrant. If the pot starts to look dry, add a splash of water.

Reduce the heat to medium-low and add the garlic, flour, salt, pepper, paprika and mustard to the pot. Stir well and let the flour cook for 1 to 2 minutes. Bring the heat up to medium-high and add the stock ½ cup at a time, stirring with a whisk between additions. Once all the stock has been added, bring up the heat so the mixture comes to a low boil. Cook for an additional 7 to 10 minutes. It will thicken as it cooks.

Add the broccoli florets and chopped carrots to the pot and stir. Cover and let the soup simmer for 15 minutes, until the carrots are fork-tender.

Add the milk and cheese, and let the soup simmer for another minute, until the cheese has completely melted. Taste and add more salt, pepper or cayenne for a kick if desired!

Divide the soup among three meal prep containers. Top with extra shredded cheese for garnish. Let them cool for a bit before covering and storing in the fridge.

Storage, Reheating and Serving Notes: This soup can last for up to 5 days in the fridge. It's not freezer friendly. Reheat this soup in the microwave or on the stove partially covered. I highly recommend enjoying it with your favorite crusty bread!

NO MICROWAVE, NO PROBLEM

Even if you don't have access to a microwave at work, you can still meal prep lunches! These no-reheat meals are perfect for on-the-go situations, or when you just want to enjoy a nice lunch outside instead of waiting in line to grab food on your lunch break.

Containers for these meals come in all shapes and sizes. You can use standard 3-cup (710-ml) containers for all of these, but you'll have an easier time prepping some of these recipes if you invest in two or three stainless steel boxes that have built-in compartments to separate the food. For wraps, I usually store them wrapped in foil in my fridge but put them in a container when eating them on the go so they don't get smushed. This chapter includes three "snack lunch" boxes, similar to what you might see in cold cases in Starbucks or airports, but way more delicious. My Soft-Boiled Egg & Smoked Salmon Snack Lunchbox recipe (page 50) is unlike anything you've seen in terms of pre-made to-go boxes, and my Tofu, Cucumber, Sweet Potato & Rice Bento (page 46) is inspired by what I learned to make in a Japanese cooking class in Tokyo where these types of lunches are common. The best no-reheat meal preps tend to be wraps, pasta salads, grain

salads and sandwiches, depending on what you fill them with. The key to meal prepping sandwiches is keeping the fillings and bread separate until you head out for work in the morning, or you can assemble them right before you eat at lunchtime. My Turmeric Chickpea Avocado Sandwiches (page 57) make this really easy to do!

Grain bowls and pasta salads make for super-reliable no-reheat meal preps. The Green Tuna Pasta Salad (page 58) was gobbled up after just two days in my household—it's that good—but it would be delicious even five days after making it. And the Chipotle Black Bean Avocado Quinoa Salad (page 54) makes a great base for additional and leftover ingredients if you have some to use up!

There are so many different wraps you could prepare for the week, and I'm so excited for you to try my Chicken Banh Mi–Inspired Wraps (page 53). My best tip for prepping wraps is to avoid wet ingredients like salsa and tomatoes. These cause wraps to get soggy. That's also why we keep the sriracha mayonnaise on the side for that recipe!

Tofu, Cucumber, Sweet Potato & Rice Bento

When I traveled to Japan, I was introduced to *bento*, which is a common lunch option for office workers and commuters. Traditionally, bentos are all about using leftovers from dinner to pack for lunch. They're meant to be eaten cold or room temperature, and they're very customizable! These bentos involve a bed of rice, crispy tofu, my all-time favorite spicy cucumber salad and roasted sweet potatoes—bonus points if you can find Japanese sweet potatoes!

Prep Time: 10 minutes | Cook Time: 20 minutes | Servings: 2

½ recipe Soy Honey Tofu (page 156)

7 oz (198 g) sweet potatoes, chopped (about 1½ cups)

1 tbsp (15 ml) olive oil

1 tsp brown sugar

1 tsp salt, divided

⅔ cup (133 g) rice

1 tsp olive oil

1⅓ cups (320 ml) water

1 heaping cup (135 g) thinly sliced cucumber

¼ cup (40 g) minced red onion

¼ cup (28 g) shredded carrot

2 scallions, green ends sliced, white ends discarded

2 tbsp (30 ml) rice vinegar

1 tbsp (15 g) sugar

2 tsp (10 ml) sesame oil

¼ tsp crushed red pepper or cayenne

2 tsp (5 g) furikake seasoning, optional

6 strawberries, halved

Preheat your oven to 400° F (200° C). Prepare the Soy Honey Tofu (page 156).

Add the sweet potatoes, olive oil, brown sugar and half the salt to a bowl. Toss together to coat well, then pour the sweet potatoes onto a baking sheet. Spread the pieces of sweet potato out and bake for 20 to 25 minutes, or until the sweet potatoes are tender. Flipping halfway through cooking is recommended.

Add the rice, olive oil, water and remaining salt to a pot over medium heat. Bring the pot to a boil, then cover with a tight-fitting lid and reduce to a simmer. Let the rice cook on the lowest heat for 10 minutes, then turn the heat off and let it steam for at least 10 minutes.

To a medium-sized bowl, add the cucumber, onion, carrot and the sliced scallions. To a small bowl, add the rice vinegar, sugar, sesame oil and red pepper. Mix well, and then pour it over the cucumber mixture and toss everything together. Set aside.

Time to assemble! Get two bentos or meal prep containers. Divide the rice among your containers and top with the furikake seasoning. Then divide and add the sweet potatoes and cucumber salad to the containers, followed by the baked tofu, leaving room for the three sliced strawberries in each container.

Storage, Reheating and Serving Notes: This bento can last in the fridge for up to 4 days and is best at room temperature or cold. If you want to reheat this and you're using a plastic or glass container, remove the cucumber salad and strawberries from the container beforehand!

Mediterranean Snack Lunchbox

This snack lunchbox is inspired by what you'd normally see in Starbucks—you know, the plastic boxes with hummus and pita? These go above and beyond with flavorful chicken, homemade hummus, olives, grapes and a chopped salad with cucumbers and tomatoes. You can assemble a sandwich from these ingredients if you'd like, or just eat it straight out of the box. This is an easy one to put together even if you don't have a special snack box with dividers.

Prep Time: 15 minutes | Cook Time: 0 minutes | Servings: 2

FOR THE SALAD

1½ cups (185 g) peeled and chopped cucumber

1 cup (149 g) cherry tomatoes, chopped

1 cup (25 g) parsley

Juice from ½ a lemon

Salt and pepper to taste

1 oz (28 g) crumbled feta cheese

FOR THE BOXES

⅔ cup (160 ml) My Go-To Hummus (page 167)

1 cup (226 g) shredded Shortcut Roasted Chicken (page 151)

1 cup (151 g) grapes

⅔ cup (118 g) kalamata olives

6–8 slices of pita bread

To a medium-sized bowl, add the cucumber, tomatoes, parsley, lemon juice, salt, pepper and feta. Toss everything together and taste to see if you need to add more salt. Set aside.

Time to assemble! Between two stainless steel containers, divided containers or regular meal prep containers, divide and arrange the chicken, salad and olives so they're next to each other. Add the grapes and hummus. To keep the pita as dry as possible, keep it on the side, or wrap it in parchment paper before adding it to the containers.

Storage, Reheating and Serving Notes: This Mediterranean Snack Lunchbox can last in the fridge for up to 4 days. It's best at room temperature or cold. The chicken can be reheated on its own if you prefer. I recommend serving these elements on a plate like a lunch platter, or you can toss the chicken, olives and salad together while enjoying pita and grapes on the side.

Soft-Boiled Egg & Smoked Salmon Snack Lunchbox

You don't have to wait for the weekend to enjoy a brunch lunch! This fun box features everything you'd want to load up on your favorite crackers: A soft-boiled egg, lox, avocado and cheese. Don't forget to add a side of fruit to balance out all the savory goodness in this box! I used cherries, but you can use any fruit you're in the mood for.

Prep Time: 5 minutes | Cook Time: 15 minutes | Servings: 2

2 eggs

1 whole avocado, mashed

1 tbsp (15 ml) lemon juice or lime juice

Salt and pepper taste

12–14 crackers of your choice

4 oz (113 g) smoked salmon, cubed

⅔ cup (99 g) feta cheese

1 cup (138 g) cherries or fruit of your choice

To soft-boil the eggs, fill a pot with enough water to submerge your eggs. Bring the water to a boil, and then carefully place the eggs in the pot. Bring the heat down to medium and cover the pot. Cook the eggs for 6 to 7 minutes for a soft egg. Meanwhile, fill a medium-sized bowl with cold water and stick it in the fridge. When the 7 minutes is up, transfer the eggs to the cold water and let them cool completely. Don't peel these until the day you plan to eat them.

Add the avocado, lemon juice, salt and pepper to a bowl. Mix well and set aside.

Time to assemble! Divide the crackers, salmon, feta and cherries between two stainless steel, plastic or glass containers, or any containers with dividers. Divide the avocado between the containers. You can keep the eggs on the side unpeeled, or you can peel the eggs and place them in the containers before heading to work to enjoy in this box.

Storage, Reheating and Serving Notes: This snack lunchbox can last in the fridge for up to 3 days. I recommend enjoying this cold or room temperature. You can build stacked crackers with egg slices, cheese, avocado and the smoked salmon, or enjoy the eggs chopped up with avocado, feta and smoked salmon to make more of an egg salad–type of mixture to spread on the crackers.

Chicken Banh Mi-Inspired Wraps

Whether you've had the pleasure of enjoying a banh mi sandwich, a Vietnamese favorite, or not, you'll want to make these easy wraps over and over. They're super easy to eat on the go, at your desk or outside if you prefer to take your lunch break enjoying some fresh air. The key to this recipe is the fresh herbs. Don't be shy with your basil and mint in these wraps!

Prep Time: 15 minutes | Cook Time: 15 minutes | Makes 3 wraps

12 oz (336 g) chicken breast, halved if it's a thick piece

¼ cup (60 ml) water

3 tbsp (45 ml) soy sauce

1 tbsp (15 ml) rice vinegar

1 tbsp (15 ml) fish sauce

2 tsp (6 g) sugar

1 tbsp (15 ml) olive oil

½ cup (120 ml) mayonnaise

1 tbsp (15 ml) sriracha, optional

3 large 10-inch (25-cm) tortillas

1½ cups (50 g) chopped lettuce or spinach

½ cup (46 g) chopped mint

½ cup (12 g) chopped basil

1 medium cucumber, sliced

1 large carrot, shredded

1 recipe Quick Pickled Red Onions (page 168), optional

Add the chicken, water, soy sauce, rice vinegar, fish sauce and sugar to a bowl. Toss well to mix everything together and set aside.

Preheat a nonstick or cast-iron skillet for a minute or two. Then add the olive oil and let it warm up. Add the chicken to the pan over medium heat and cook on each side for 3 to 4 minutes, until the chicken is cooked through and has darkened in color. You may need to cook the chicken in two batches to avoid crowding the pan. Set the chicken aside and let it cool completely. When the chicken has cooled, chop it roughly to make it easier to wrap. Mix the mayonnaise and sriracha in a small sealable container and set it aside.

To assemble the wraps, lay a tortilla on a flat surface. Add ½ cup (17 g) of lettuce in a horizontal layer on the lower third section of the tortilla. Add one-third of the mint and one-third of the basil leaves on top of the lettuce. Add one-third of the cucumber in a flat layer, topped with one-third of the shredded carrot. Top the carrot with one-third of the chopped chicken. If using Quick Pickled Onions (page 168), add 3 to 4 on top of the chicken.

To roll, fold the bottom of the tortilla up over the fillings—it won't come completely over and that's okay. Fold the two sides of the tortilla over the fillings inward. Roll the wrap away from you, keeping the sides tucked in, until completely rolled up. If you need help, I recommend watching a quick video online for how to do this!

Repeat the last two steps for the remaining two wraps. Store the wraps, uncut, in foil or saran wrap, or place directly in a container. If the wrap is falling apart, you can use toothpicks to hold it together. Keep the sriracha mayonnaise on the side in small dressing containers until ready to eat, when you'll drizzle it on as you eat.

Storage, Reheating and Serving Notes: These banh mi-inspired wraps last for up to 4 days in the fridge and taste great cold or room temperature!

Chipotle Black Bean Avocado Quinoa Salad

Grain bowls are the real MVP of no-reheat lunches. There are endless ways to customize them. This bowl is satisfying, has a little bit of a kick and requires almost no cooking! This salad would be a great base for extra protein you have from other meals too. You can eat it cold, room temperature or slightly warm if you'd like!

Prep Time: 15 minutes | Cook Time: 15 minutes | Servings: 3

⅔ cup (112 g) quinoa, rinsed

1 tsp salt, divided

½ tsp ground pepper, divided

1 tsp chili powder

1 tsp garlic powder (sub 2 cloves fresh garlic, minced)

1⅓ cups (320 ml) vegetable broth (sub water)

1 (15-oz [420-ml] can black beans, rinsed and drained

1 cup (149 g) cherry tomatoes, chopped

⅔ cup (96 g) chopped red onion

3 radishes, chopped in half and sliced

1 cup (16 g) chopped cilantro (keep the stems)

3 cups (100 g) chopped spinach

3 scallions, white and green ends chopped and separated

1 avocado, chopped

1 lime, halved

2 chipotle peppers in adobo sauce, chopped and seeded

3 tsp (15 ml) adobo sauce (from can of peppers)

2 tbsp (30 ml) mayonnaise

1 tbsp (15 ml) water, to thin

Tortilla chips, for serving

Add the quinoa, half of the salt and pepper, chili powder, garlic powder and vegetable broth to a pot over high heat. Bring the pot to a boil, then cover and reduce to a simmer. Allow the quinoa to simmer for 12 to 15 minutes, or until it has absorbed all of the water and fluffs easily with a fork.

Meanwhile, add the black beans, cherry tomatoes, red onion, radishes, cilantro, spinach and green ends of the scallions to a bowl. Add the chopped avocado on top and squeeze half a lime directly onto the avocado. Mix gently.

To a food processor, add the white ends of the scallions, chipotle peppers, adobo sauce, mayonnaise and water. Add the remaining salt and pepper. Blend until smooth and creamy. You should still see some small pieces of chipotle pepper.

Add the quinoa and chipotle sauce to the bowl with the veggies and juice from the remaining lime half. Toss everything together. Divide the mixture among three meal prep containers. Keep the tortilla chips on the side until you eat.

Storage, Reheating and Serving Notes: This meal lasts for up to 4 days in the fridge. It's not freezer friendly. You can eat this meal cold, at room temperature or heated in the microwave or on the stove.

Turmeric Chickpea Avocado Sandwiches

This no-cook, no-reheat wonder is so satisfying to enjoy at lunch! They're so fast to make too. The key to meal prepping any sandwich is keeping the fillings and bread separate, and then you assemble the sandwich right before you eat. This chickpea avocado mash is easy to pack up, store and take on the go. You can use it on a bagel, in a wrap or on pita bread instead of regular sandwich bread if you're looking to change it up!

Prep Time: 15 minutes | Cook Time: 0 minutes | Servings: 3

1 (15-oz [420-ml]) can chickpeas, rinsed and drained

1 avocado, mashed

1 tsp turmeric

½ tsp curry powder

¼ tsp cayenne, optional

Salt and pepper to taste

2 tbsp (30 ml) lemon juice

⅓ cup (80 ml) mayonnaise, optional

1 tbsp (15 ml) sriracha or chili garlic sauce, optional

2 cups (66 g) spinach, roughly chopped

1 Roma tomato, sliced

6–9 red onion slices

6 slices of sandwich bread of your choice

Cheese and any of your favorite sandwich fixings, optional

Add the chickpeas to a bowl and mash with a fork or masher. Then add the mashed avocado, turmeric, curry powder, cayenne, if using, salt, pepper and lemon juice. Mash well and mix to make sure the lemon juice is fully incorporated. Taste and add more salt or pepper as needed.

Mix the mayonnaise and sriracha together, if using, to make spicy mayonnaise and set aside in one container or three smaller dressing containers until ready to eat.

Store the chickpea avocado mash separate from the spinach, tomato, onion slices, bread and other sandwich fixings.

To assemble and eat, spread a tablespoon or more of spicy mayonnaise on one slice of fresh or toasted bread. Add a layer of spinach to your bread, followed by ⅓ to ½ cup (80 to 120 g) of chickpea avocado mash, sliced tomato and sliced onion. Spread another tablespoon of spicy mayonnaise on the other slice of bread and place it mayonnaise-side down on top of the onion.

Storage, Reheating and Serving Notes: The chickpea avocado mash lasts for up to 4 days in the fridge when kept separate from the spinach, tomato and onion. It's not freezer friendly. Spicy mayonnaise lasts for at least a week in the fridge. Bread can be frozen and thawed, kept in the fridge or on the counter. I recommend eating this cold or at room temperature!

Green Tuna Pasta Salad

Confession: I've never been a huge tuna person, but this recipe converted me. I crave this easy pasta salad constantly and it's a great lunch for work. If you're not into asparagus, you can swap it out for any vegetable that tastes good blanched, like broccoli or green beans. If you wanted to make this vegan, you can swap tuna out for chickpeas, but it won't have the same savory flavor profile. It's really all about the sauce! This recipe is perfect for using up herbs on their last legs. Use whatever you have on hand!

Prep Time: 10 minutes | Cook Time: 15 minutes | Servings: 3

12 oz (336 g) asparagus, chopped into bite-sized pieces, ends discarded

6 oz (170 g) bowtie pasta (about 2 cups)

½ tsp salt, plus more as needed

½ cup (13 g) parsley

½ cup (15 g) basil

½ cup (8 g) cilantro

½ lemon, for juice

1 tbsp (15 ml) Dijon mustard

2 cloves garlic

⅓ cup (80 ml) plain Greek yogurt

⅔ cup (100 g) avocado (about ½ a large avocado)

¼ cup (60 ml) water

¼ tsp ground pepper

2 (5-oz [142-ml]) cans of tuna packed in oil, drained

⅓ cup (18 g) sun-dried tomatoes, chopped

½ cup (80 g) chopped red onion (sub shallots)

Bring a large pot of water to boil. Add the asparagus and pasta to the water at the same time, with a generous pinch of salt. Continue to cook until the pasta is cooked through, and then drain and cover the pasta and asparagus with a lid until ready to use.

In a food processor, add the parsley, basil, cilantro, juice from half a lemon, mustard, garlic, Greek yogurt, avocado, water, salt and pepper. Process until smooth, scraping down the sides as needed, for about 5 minutes until smooth.

To a large bowl, add the cooked pasta, asparagus, tuna, sun-dried tomatoes, red onion and blended sauce. Toss well to mix everything together.

Divide the pasta salad among three meal prep containers.

Storage, Reheating and Serving Notes: This pasta salad lasts for up to 4 days in the fridge. It's best to eat cold or at room temperature, but you can reheat it in the microwave if you want. This meal is not freezer friendly.

BOWLS WITH SOUL

There's just something about eating a meal in a bowl. It's comforting and so much easier to mix all the yummy ingredients together! Plus, the customizations for bowl meals are endless. You've probably come across bowl meals online and in fast casual takeout spots. Meals like vegan Buddha bowls and burrito bowls—check out our amazing take on this lunch classic with our Mission-Style Steak Burrito Bowls (page 65)—have become increasingly popular, and for a good reason! Bowl meals are the best.

For these recipes, any type of container you have will work. Plastic boxes, circular glass containers—whatever you have will be a great vessel for your bowl meals, as long as it's microwave safe. If you're working from home, I recommend transferring these meals into a real bowl from the container to make your lunch feel even fancier.

This chapter contains bowl meals featuring different grains and types of pasta as the base and each of them has a different flavor profile to get you inspired. I can bet that your coworkers will be jealous when they see you pull these out of the office fridge!

The bowl meal prep formula is easy to remember. You need a base, usually a grain like farro, which we use in our Chickpea Halloumi Farro Bowls (page 71), two to three different types of vegetables to get a variety in texture and protein to keep you full and energized through the afternoon. Topping it off with a sauce or dressing makes it even better, like our Creamy Avocado Herb Sauce (page 160) on the Chicken Kahti Roll-Inspired Bowls (page 68).

Bowl meals are my favorite for meal prep because they're probably one of the easiest types of meals to reheat. They all last up to 5 days in the fridge, too, making them a perfect option for work lunches. All you have to do is stick them in the microwave or reheat them on the stove. You can even eat these at room temperature and they'll still be delicious! The Honey Chipotle Shrimp Quinoa Bowls (page 72) chilled right out of the fridge is especially refreshing.

Italian Turkey Meatball Orzo Bowls

I have an obsession with orzo. It's one of the most underrated pastas out there and perfect for bowl meals if you're tired of rice and grains! Meatballs are an incredible meal prep staple, too, because you can make a lot of them at once and they freeze like a dream. This meal looks gorgeous when assembled in sections (pictured) but tastes the best when you mix everything together.

Prep Time: 10 minutes | Cook Time: 25 minutes | Servings: 3

FOR THE BOWLS

2 cups (298 g) cherry tomatoes

2 tbsp (30 ml) olive oil, divided

Salt and pepper to taste

1 cup (112 g) orzo

1 tbsp (14 g) butter

2 cups (227 g) sliced baby bella mushrooms

Extra chopped parsley, for garnish

½ cup (50 g) grated Parmesan cheese

FOR THE ITALIAN TURKEY MEATBALLS

Cooking spray

¼ cup (60 ml) milk

1 egg

½ cup (28 g) breadcrumbs

¼ cup (15 g) chopped parsley

¼ cup (25 g) grated Parmesan cheese

1 tbsp (15 ml) ketchup

2 tsp (10 ml) extra virgin olive oil

2 cloves garlic, minced

½ onion, chopped finely

½ tsp salt

¼ tsp ground pepper

1 lb (454 g) ground turkey

Preheat your oven to 400°F (200°C).

For the bowls, add the cherry tomatoes, 1 tablespoon (15 ml) of olive oil and salt and pepper to taste to a sheet pan. Toss with your hands to coat and bake for 20 to 25 minutes, until the tomatoes have burst and are slightly caramelized.

In a medium pot, cook the orzo according to the package. When it's done cooking, drain and add the butter and a pinch of salt. Cover the orzo when it's done to keep it from drying out.

For the meatballs, spray a second sheet pan with cooking spray and set aside. To a large bowl, add the milk and egg, and whisk. Then add the breadcrumbs, parsley, Parmesan cheese, ketchup, extra virgin olive oil, garlic, onion, salt and pepper. Mix everything together well with a wooden spoon or spatula, and then add the ground turkey and mix again until well combined.

Optional Step: Heat up a small skillet on the stove and spray with cooking spray. Add about 2 teaspoons (10 g) of the meatball mixture and let it cook through (4 to 5 minutes over medium heat). Taste the cooked piece of meatball and adjust flavors as needed. You may want to add more salt, pepper or parsley.

Shape the turkey meatballs (2 to 3 tablespoons [30 to 45 ml] per ball) and place them on the sheet pan. Make sure they're not touching. I got 20 meatballs from this recipe. Bake for 20 to 22 minutes, until the meatballs have browned in the oven and are firm to the touch.

(continued)

Italian Turkey Meatball Orzo Bowls (continued)

1 cup (225 g) marinara sauce

Preheat a large skillet over medium heat for 1 to 2 minutes. Add the remaining olive oil and let it heat for 1 minute, and then add the sliced mushrooms with a generous pinch of salt and pepper to taste. Cook, stirring gently every few minutes, for about 15 minutes over medium heat until the mushrooms have shrunk down in size and are very fragrant. If the pan looks dry while cooking, add a splash of water to the mushrooms. When the mushrooms are done, remove them from the pan and set aside. Return the pan to the stove.

When the meatballs are done, add them to the skillet you used for the mushrooms along with the marinara sauce over low heat. Toss gently to coat the meatballs in the sauce.

Divide the orzo among three meal prep containers. Top with the tomatoes, mushrooms and meatballs. Garnish with extra parsley and grated Parmesan cheese.

Storage, Reheating and Serving Notes: This meal lasts for 4 days in the fridge. It's not freezer friendly. Reheat the entire meal prep container in the microwave when you're ready to eat. Alternatively, reheat the entire meal in a pan on the stove with a little oil or water to prevent sticking.

Mission-Style Steak Burrito Bowls

The first time I visited my brother in San Francisco, he picked me up from the airport and took me directly to the Mission District to try a burrito. The Mission District is known for its incredible loaded meat burritos, piled high with sour cream, avocado and pico de gallo, all bundled up in a warm homemade flour tortilla. They're massive, delicious and somewhat life-changing! I miss San Francisco so much and had to recreate these famous burritos in bowl form. Burrito bowls are a popular takeout lunch, but you won't find anything like this bowl at Chipotle.

Prep Time: 15 minutes | Cook Time: 30 minutes | Servings: 3

FOR THE CARNE ASADA

½ cup (120 ml) orange or grapefruit juice

¼ cup (60 ml) lime juice

¼ cup (60 ml) lemon juice

¼ cup (60 ml) olive oil

2 tsp (10 ml) honey or white sugar

1 clove garlic, minced

1 tsp cumin

½ tsp chili powder

½ tsp salt

¼ tsp ground black pepper

½ tsp cayenne, optional

1 lb (454 g) flank steak, cut into 2 big pieces

¼ cup (60 ml) vegetable oil, for cooking

FOR THE RICE

1 tsp olive oil

¾ cup (50 g) white rice

½ cup (90 g) salsa

1 cup (240 ml) water

¼ tsp salt

To a measuring glass, add the orange juice, lime juice, lemon juice, olive oil, honey, garlic, cumin, chili powder, salt, pepper and cayenne, if you like heat. Stir well to combine the ingredients, taste and add more salt or pepper if necessary. Place the flank steak in a ziplock bag or deep glass container. Pour the marinade on top and let it sit for 20 minutes if cooking right away, or up to 24 hours in the fridge, covered.

Heat up a pot on the stove for a minute or two, then add the oil and rice. Toast the rice over medium-high heat, stirring occasionally, for 1 to 2 minutes. Then add the salsa, water and salt. Stir once and bring up the heat. When the rice boils, reduce the heat to a simmer and cover the pot. Let it cook for 10 minutes. Turn off the heat and let the rice steam for another 10 minutes. Before assembling your meal preps, fluff the rice with a fork.

(continued)

Mission-Style Steak Burrito Bowls (continued)

FOR THE BEANS

1 tbsp olive oil

2 cloves garlic, minced

1 (15-oz [420-ml]) can pinto beans, rinsed and drained

½ tsp cumin

Salt and pepper to taste

TOPPINGS

Mashed avocado

Sour cream

Pico de gallo

Lime wedges, for garnish

Cilantro, for garnish

For the beans, heat up a skillet over medium heat for a minute, then add the olive oil and garlic. Stir for a minute, then add the pinto beans, cumin, salt and pepper. Cook for 7 to 10 minutes over medium heat, stirring occasionally, until the beans are soft and seasoned.

Heat up a cast-iron skillet for 3 to 4 minutes, until it's very hot but not smoking. Add the vegetable oil and let it warm up for 2 to 3 minutes. Using tongs, remove one piece of steak from the marinade and place it on the skillet carefully. It should sizzle loudly. Let it cook for 4 to 5 minutes over medium-high heat, then flip it and cook for another 3 to 4 minutes. If you have a meat thermometer, the internal temperature should be 135 to 140°F (55 to 40°C) when it's ready to be taken off the heat. If not, press your finger to the steak and push down. It should give a little but shouldn't be completely firm or very tender. Transfer the steak to a cutting board and let it rest for 10 to 15 minutes. Meanwhile, repeat the above with the other piece of steak.

To assemble your meals, divide the cooked rice among three meal prep containers as the bottom layer. Add the cooked beans on top. Chop the rested steak into small cubes and divide among your containers. Keep your toppings on the side until serving.

> **Storage, Reheating and Serving Notes:** This recipe lasts for up to 4 days in the fridge and isn't freezer friendly. I recommend reheating the rice, beans and steak in the microwave or on the stove. Then add as much avocado, pico de gallo, sour cream and other toppings as you want before eating.

Chicken Kahti Roll–Inspired Bowls

If you ever have the chance to order a kahti roll at an Indian restaurant, do it! These rolls are made with a fried egg, yogurt-marinated chicken, sauces and veggies all bundled up in a warm paratha. The bowl version, inspired by the wrap, incorporates similar flavors and textures.

Prep Time: 20 minutes | Cook Time: 40 minutes | Servings: 3–4

½ cup (120 ml) plain Greek yogurt

1 tbsp (15 ml) olive oil

2 tsp (5g) turmeric, divided

2 tsp (5g) garam masala, divided

1-inch (2.5-cm) piece ginger, minced, divided

4 cloves garlic, minced, divided

1 tsp cumin

½ tsp chili powder

½ tsp salt

¼ tsp ground pepper

1 lb (425 g) boneless, skinless chicken thighs, chopped

1 tbsp (15 g) butter or olive oil

⅔ cup (133 g) rice

1 cup (134 g) frozen peas

1⅓ cups (320 ml) chicken stock or water

2 tbsp (30 ml) vegetable oil, divided

½ cup (80 g) chopped yellow onion (about ½ an onion)

1 red bell pepper, sliced

TOPPINGS

Creamy Avocado Herb Sauce (page 160), optional

Quick Pickled Onions (page 168), optional

1 cup (16 g) cilantro

In a medium-sized bowl, mix the yogurt, olive oil, half of the turmeric, half of the garam masala, half of the ginger, half of the garlic, cumin, chili powder, salt and pepper. Add the chicken thighs and toss well to coat it in the yogurt mix. Set aside.

In a pot over medium heat, add the butter and let it melt. Add the rice, remaining turmeric, garam masala, ginger and garlic, frozen peas and chicken stock. Stir well, then bring the mixture to a boil. Reduce the heat to a simmer and cover the pot with a tight-fitting lid. Let the rice cook on the lowest heat for 10 minutes, then turn off the heat and let it steam for at least 10 minutes.

Preheat a cast-iron skillet over medium heat. Add half of the vegetable oil and let it warm up for a few minutes. Add the onion and red bell pepper with salt and pepper. Cook over high heat for 7 to 10 minutes, stirring often, until the bell pepper is soft and slightly charred on the edges. Remove the vegetables from the skillet and set aside.

In the same skillet, add the remaining vegetable oil over medium heat. Using tongs, transfer the chicken from the bowl to the pan, aiming to not get too much marinade in the pan. You may need to cook the chicken in two batches to avoid crowding the pan. Cook the chicken over medium heat for about 12 minutes, rotating the pieces every few minutes, until it's completely cooked through and has lots of color on the edges. Set the chicken aside. If making the Creamy Avocado Herb Sauce (page 160), prepare it at this point. Divide the sauce among three small containers for dressings and set aside.

To assemble these meal preps, divide the rice among three meal prep containers. Then divide the cooked bell pepper and onion and the chicken among the containers. If using Quick Pickled Red Onions, add them to the containers as well. Garnish with cilantro. Keep the creamy herb sauce on the side until you eat!

Storage and Reheating Notes: This bowl can last in the fridge for up to 4 days. It's not freezer friendly. Reheat it then add a few dollops of the creamy herb sauce on top!

Chickpea Halloumi Farro Bowls

This bowl is an upgraded version of the classic "Buddha Bowl" that generally involves chickpeas, a grain, roasted veggies and a sauce. The halloumi takes it to a whole other level. Don't be intimidated by halloumi! It's so easy to pan-fry. If you can't find it, I recommend using feta or paneer instead. And you can easily swap out the brussels sprouts and broccolini for any oven-friendly veggie, like bell peppers, eggplant, tomatoes and beets.

Prep Time: 10 minutes | Cook Time: 40 minutes | Servings: 3

3 cups (720 ml) vegetable broth or water

1 cup (166 g) pearled farro, or grain of your choice

1½ tsp (4 g) salt, divided

¾ tsp ground pepper, divided

4 tbsp (60 ml) olive oil, divided

2 cups (200 g) brussels sprouts, halved

1 bunch broccolini or broccoli, chopped into florets

2 cloves garlic, minced

1 (15-oz [420-ml]) can chickpeas, rinsed and drained

1 tsp paprika

4 oz (113 g) halloumi, sliced into ½-inch (1.3-cm) slabs

1 large carrot, julienned or shredded

1 recipe All-Purpose Tahini Lemon Sauce (page 163), for serving, optional

Storage, Reheating and Serving Notes: These bowls can last in the fridge for 3 to 4 days. They're not freezer friendly. You can reheat them in the microwave or on the stove. Keep the tahini sauce on the side until you eat!

Preheat your oven to 400°F (200°C)

Add the vegetable broth to a pot and bring it to a boil. Add in the farro along with a ½ teaspoon of salt and a ¼ teaspoon of pepper and bring the pot to a simmer. Cook for 15 to 20 minutes, until the farro is tender and chewy.

Add 1 tablespoon (15 ml) of the olive oil to a bowl with the brussels sprouts and ½ teaspoon of salt and ¼ teaspoon of pepper and toss well. Then pour the brussels sprouts onto a baking sheet. Flip the brussels so they're cut side down on the pan. Bake for 15 to 20 minutes, until the edges are slightly brown. Then, flip them over and bake for an additional 5 to 10 minutes, until they have caramelized around the edges.

Add another tablespoon (15 ml) of olive oil to the same bowl along with the broccolini, minced garlic, remaining salt and pepper. Toss well to coat, and then pour onto another baking sheet. Push the broccolini to one side to make room for the chickpeas.

Add one more tablespoon (15 ml) of olive oil to the bowl along with the chickpeas, paprika, ½ teaspoon of salt and ¼ teaspoon of pepper. Pour the chickpeas onto the baking sheet next to the broccolini. Cook for 10 to 12 minutes in the oven, until the chickpeas are slightly crispy and the broccolini is fork tender.

Heat up a grill pan or skillet over medium heat for a minute or two. Add the remaining olive oil, then add the halloumi to the pan. Let it cook on each side for 2 to 3 minutes, or until it's golden in color in some places. Remove it from the pan, and then let it cool before slicing into smaller pieces, if desired.

If making the All-Purpose Tahini Lemon Sauce, prepare it at this point. Divide the sauce among three small containers for dressings and set aside.

To assemble your meal preps, divide the farro among three meal prep containers. Then divide the brussels sprouts, broccolini, chickpeas, shredded carrot and halloumi among the bowls.

Honey Chipotle Shrimp Quinoa Bowls

This meal is deceptively easy and great for a lighter lunch. It has that spicy smokiness that tastes like summer, balanced with the sweetness from the coconut milk. You'll love this coconut milk–based chipotle sauce with any protein in case you're not a shrimp fan. This meal is great as a cold or room temperature lunch, too, in case you're on the go or don't feel like waiting in line for the microwave. The key to meal prepping shrimp is not overcooking it, so keep an eye on it when you're putting this together!

Prep Time: 15 minutes | Cook Time: 25 minutes | Servings: 3

1 cup (170 g) quinoa, rinsed

1 cup (240 ml) water

½ cup (90 g) salsa, plus more for serving

2 cloves garlic, minced

1 tsp salt, divided

3 chipotle peppers in adobo sauce, roughly chopped and deseeded

2 tsp (10 ml) adobo sauce (from can of peppers)

1 cup (16 g) cilantro, divided

½ cup (120 ml) honey

½ tsp chili powder

1 lb (454 g) shrimp, peeled and deveined

1 tbsp (15 ml) vegetable oil

1 orange bell pepper, chopped

1 cup (136 g) frozen corn, thawed

1 lime, cut into wedges

Sliced avocado, for topping, optional

To a pot, add the quinoa, water, salsa, minced garlic and half of the salt. Bring to a boil, then reduce the heat, cover the pot and simmer until the liquid is gone. Keep covered until ready to use.

To a food processor, add the chipotle peppers, adobo sauce, half of the cilantro, honey, remaining salt and chili powder. Process until smooth.

Pat the shrimp dry. Then place the shrimp in a bowl and add the chipotle mixture. Toss the shrimp gently to coat it in the marinade.

Heat up a nonstick skillet over medium heat. Then add the vegetable oil and let it warm up for a minute or two. Add the shrimp to the pan in a single layer with the remaining marinade and cook on each side for 3 to 4 minutes, until the shrimp curls up and is bright pink in color. Add the bell pepper and corn, stir and cook for an additional 3 to 5 minutes over medium-high heat, until the corn is warmed through.

Divide the quinoa among three meal prep containers. Top with the shrimp and bell pepper mixture and more salsa. Garnish with cilantro leaves and lime wedges. Keep the avocado on the side until you eat, and give the bowl a squeeze of lime before digging in.

Storage, Reheating and Serving Notes: This meal lasts for 4 days in the fridge. It's not freezer friendly. Reheat the entire meal prep container in the microwave when you're ready to eat. Alternatively, reheat the entire meal in a pan on the stove with a little oil or water to prevent sticking.

Mango Tofu & Coconut Rice Bowls

Coconut rice and mango are one of my favorite combos, and they come together for a satisfying and flavorful lunch in this recipe. If you want to speed this recipe up even more, you could bake the tofu instead of panfrying it.

Prep Time: 15 minutes | Cook Time: 40 minutes | Servings: 3–4

¾ cup (150 g) rice

1 cup (240 ml) coconut milk

½ cup (120 ml) water

½ tsp salt

1 lime

¼ cup (60 ml) honey

¼ cup (60 ml) soy sauce

2 tsp (10 ml) sriracha, optional

1 (14-oz [392-ml]) package of firm tofu, drained and pressed

2 tbsp (16 g) cornstarch

Salt to taste

3 tbsp (45 ml) vegetable oil, divided

1 zucchini, chopped

1 mango, peeled and chopped

1 jalapeño, seeded and chopped, optional

½ cup (8 g) cilantro, optional

2 tbsp (18 g) sesame seeds, optional

Lime wedges, optional

Add the rice, coconut milk, water and salt to a pot over high heat. Bring the pot to a boil, then cover and reduce to a simmer. Cook for 10 minutes over low heat, then turn off the heat and let it sit for another 10 minutes. Then fluff with a fork and let it sit, covered. Zest the lime with a microplane or grater—you need ½ teaspoon. Then cut the lime in half. Juice one half of the lime and cut the other half into wedges.

To a measuring glass, add the honey, soy sauce, sriracha (if using) and lime zest, plus juice from half of the lime. Mix the soy-honey mixture well, taste it and adjust the flavors to your preference.

Heat up a large nonstick skillet over medium heat. Chop the tofu into cubes and place them in a bowl. Sprinkle the cornstarch and salt on the tofu and toss gently to coat. Add half of the vegetable oil to the skillet and let it warm up for a minute or two. Then add the tofu to the pan, making sure to avoid overcrowding it—you may need to cook the tofu in two batches. Cook on each side for about 5 minutes over medium heat, until the edges are crispy and golden in color. Set aside when you've cooked all of the tofu.

Add the remaining oil to the skillet, along with the zucchini and salt to taste. Add 1 tablespoon (15 ml) of the honey-soy mixture to the pan and sauté the zucchini for about 10 minutes, stirring often, until it's fork-tender. Remove the zucchini from the pan.

Add the remaining honey-soy mixture to the skillet over medium heat and let it cook for about 5 minutes, until it starts to thicken. If this process is taking a while, turn up the heat. Add the tofu and zucchini back to the pan and toss to coat it in the sauce. Turn off the heat and stir in the mango and jalapeño, if using.

Divide the cooked rice among three meal prep containers. Add the tofu-mango-zucchini mixture on top. Garnish with cilantro, lime wedges and sesame seeds, if desired.

Storage, Reheating and Serving Notes: This meal lasts for up to 4 days in the fridge. It's not freezer friendly.

Moroccan-Inspired Salmon Couscous Bowls

This is a fun, flavorful twist on one of my classic meal preps, roasted salmon and veggies. Couscous is one of the easiest carb elements to prep since it usually takes about 5 minutes to prepare and reheats very well. Remix this meal by using the ingredients in a stuffed pepper or cheesy spaghetti squash—trust me—or add greens to make it into more of a salad!

Prep Time: 10 minutes | Cook Time: 30 minutes | Servings: 3

FOR THE BOWLS

1 medium eggplant, peeled and chopped into bite-sized pieces

1 small cauliflower, chopped into florets

2 carrots, diagonally chopped into 1-inch (2.5-cm) pieces

½ cup (80 g) chopped yellow onion (about ½ an onion)

2 cloves garlic, minced

1 tsp salt

½ tsp ground pepper

1 tsp cumin

2 tbsp (30 ml) olive oil

⅔ cup (113 g) couscous

1 cup (60 g) chopped parsley

1 lemon, chopped into wedges

1 recipe All-Purpose Tahini Lemon Sauce (page 163), optional

FOR THE SALMON

½ tsp cumin

½ tsp turmeric

½ tsp paprika

¼ tsp allspice

¼ tsp cinnamon

¼ tsp ground pepper

½ tsp salt

2 tbsp (30 ml) olive oil

2 tsp (10 ml) honey

1 lb (454 g) salmon, cut into 3 pieces

Preheat your oven to 425°F (220°C).

To a bowl, add the eggplant, cauliflower, carrots, onion, garlic, salt, pepper, cumin and olive oil. Toss the vegetables well to coat them in the spices and oil, and then pour the mixture onto a baking sheet. You can use two baking sheets if needed. Bake for 25 to 27 minutes, flipping the veggies halfway through, until they're very soft and have darkened in color around the edges. If your eggplant tastes bitter, it needs more time in the oven.

For the salmon, mix the cumin, turmeric, paprika, allspice, cinnamon, ground pepper and salt in a small bowl. Add the olive oil and stir. Place a sheet of parchment paper or a silicone mat on a baking sheet and place the salmon on top skin side down. Rub the spice blend on the top and sides of the salmon and bake for 15 to 20 minutes, or until the salmon is firm to the touch and flakes apart. A meat thermometer will read 140°F (60°C) when it's ready to come out of the oven.

Prepare the couscous according to the package. If making the All-Purpose Tahini Sauce, prepare it at this point. Divide the sauce among three small containers for dressings and set aside.

Divide the couscous among three meal prep containers. Top with the cooked roasted vegetables and salmon. Garnish with parsley and lemon wedges.

Storage, Reheating and Serving Notes: This meal lasts for up to 4 days in the fridge. It's not freezer friendly. Remove the lemon wedge and reheat in the microwave or in a pan on the stove with a little oil/water to prevent sticking. When you're ready to eat, then squeeze the lemon over the salmon.

HAPPY SALADS

No sad salads here! Happy salads only.

When I first started meal prepping, I attempted to make a crunchy, crispy and fresh Greek salad many times, only to end up with the soggiest lunch you've ever seen. I made the mistake of using juicy Roma tomatoes, which tend to make everything in your meal prep container soggy and wet. Luckily, I've perfected My Favorite Spinach Greek Salad (page 93) over the years and cracked the code to meal prepping many other salads that hold up very well in the fridge for a few days.

I like using deep containers for salads that hold 30 oz (887 ml) or more because it gives the ingredients a little more room to breathe. Plus, there's extra room to shake up the salad with your dressing before you eat or just to mix it up.

Salads can be hit or miss for prep, but here are the two most important tips. You never want to pre-dress your salad. Always keep your dressing on the side, especially for salads you want to stay crisp, like our Crunchy Mandarin Salad with Salmon (page 89). And you always want to let ingredients cool completely before assembling your salads. If they're warm, your greens will start to wilt!

Another tricky part of prepping salads is choosing the right greens to use. I tend to stick to kale and spinach because they're reliable in the fridge and can hold up well for a few days compared to romaine. We use iceberg lettuce in the Jerk Shrimp, Corn & Black Bean Salad (page 86) and the Thai-Inspired Tofu Chopped Salad (page 83) for the extra crunch, and that holds up well too!

I personally love making my own salad dressings. Every recipe in this chapter has a dressing recipe to go with it, but you can totally use pre-made dressings if that's your preference. One dressing not to skip is in the Loaded Kale Caesar Chicken Salad recipe (page 90). It's so good and can go with many different meals or be used as a dip!

Butternut Squash Chickpea Kale Salad

You don't have to wait until the holidays to enjoy these fall flavors! This butternut squash and apple salad with a kale base has it all. Topped with crunchy pepitas and soft, salty feta with our go-to mustard dressing on top, you'll feel like you're at an airy cafe instead of your work desk when you eat this meal. This salad tastes great cold, room temperature or even slightly warmed up! You can easily turn it into a fall wrap if you're not in the mood for salad one day—just add a tortilla!

Prep Time: 10 minutes | Cook Time: 40 minutes | Servings: 3

FOR THE COOKED VEGGIES

Cooking spray

2 tbsp (30 ml) olive oil, divided

1 lb (454 g) butternut squash, peeled and chopped into cubes

¼ cup (60 ml) maple syrup

1 tsp salt, divided

½ tsp pepper, divided

1 (15-oz [420-ml]) can chickpeas, rinsed and drained

½ tsp allspice

½ tsp paprika

1½ tsp (4 g) cumin

FOR THE DRESSING

¼ cup (80 ml) honey

¼ cup (80 ml) Dijon mustard

¼ cup (80 ml) olive oil

1 tbsp (15 ml) Worcestershire or soy sauce

1 tbsp (15 ml) water

2 tbsp (30 ml) lemon juice

Salt and pepper to taste

¼ tsp crushed red pepper flakes, optional

Preheat your oven to 400°F (200°C). Prepare two baking sheets with cooking spray.

Add 1 tablespoon (15 ml) of the olive oil, butternut squash, maple syrup, half of the salt and half of the pepper to a bowl and mix well to coat the squash. Using a slotted spoon, transfer the butternut squash onto a baking sheet and roast for 30 to 35 minutes, flipping halfway, until the squash is soft and caramelized around the edges. Let the squash cool after roasting.

In the same bowl, add the chickpeas, allspice, paprika, cumin, remaining salt, remaining pepper and remaining olive oil. Toss well to coat the chickpeas and pour the mixture onto a second baking sheet. Bake for 10 to 15 minutes, shaking the pan halfway to rotate the chickpeas. They're done when they're slightly firm and golden in color. Let the chickpeas cool after roasting.

Meanwhile, prepare the dressing. Combine the honey, Dijon mustard, olive oil, Worcestershire sauce, water, lemon juice, salt and pepper to taste and crushed red pepper flakes, if desired. Use a fork to stir the ingredients until smooth and combined. Taste and adjust flavors to your preferences. Store it in three small containers for dressings and set aside.

(continued)

Butternut Squash Chickpea Kale Salad (continued)

FOR THE SALAD

1 Honeycrisp apple, sliced

1 tbsp (15 ml) lemon juice

4 cups (268 g) chopped kale

1½ tbsp (23 ml) olive oil

½ tsp salt

¾ cup (113 g) goat cheese or feta cheese

⅔ cup (92 g) pepitas

Toss the sliced apples in a bowl with the lemon juice and set aside. This helps keep them from going brown when stored in the fridge!

In a bowl, add the kale, olive oil and salt. Massage the olive oil into the kale for a few minutes, until the kale is bright green and softer to the touch.

To assemble the salads, get three meal prep containers ready. Divide the kale among the containers, followed by the apples, cooked squash, chickpeas, goat cheese and pepitas. Keep the dressing on the side until you eat.

Storage, Reheating and Serving Notes: This salad can last in the fridge for up to 4 days. It's great cold or at room temperature. Enjoy with a drizzle of this delicious dressing or your favorite dressing, if you'd prefer!

Thai-Inspired Tofu Chopped Salad

This salad is all about texture! Featuring crisp fresh vegetables, crunchy peanuts, tasty tofu and a silky peanut butter–based dressing, you'll look forward to this colorful vegan lunch all week. You can easily swap out tofu for chicken or shrimp if you eat meat. To switch up this meal, I recommend doing away with the lettuce and turning it into a stir-fry over the Coconut Rice (page 149) by quickly sautéing the vegetables on the stove and using the dressing as a sauce, or turning the salad into a wrap.

Prep Time: 20 minutes | Cook Time: 20 minutes | Servings: 3

FOR THE TOFU

1 (14-oz [392-ml]) package of firm tofu, drained, pressed and chopped into cubes

Cooking spray

2 tbsp (30 g) peanut or nut butter of your choice

2 tbsp (30 ml) soy sauce

1 tbsp (15 ml) agave or honey, plus more to taste

1 tbsp (15 ml) rice vinegar

2 tsp (10 ml) chili garlic sauce or sriracha

1 tsp sesame oil

FOR THE SALAD

4 cups (288 g) romaine lettuce, roughly chopped

1 red bell pepper, sliced into strips

2 carrots, chopped into matchsticks or peeled into ribbons

1½ cups (105 g) shredded red cabbage

1 cup (16 g) chopped cilantro

Preheat your oven to 400°F (200°C). Let the tofu press for 10 to 30 minutes before using. Prepare a sheet pan with cooking spray.

To a measuring glass, add the peanut butter, soy sauce, agave, rice vinegar, chili garlic sauce and sesame oil. Stir well, taste and adjust flavors to your preference. Set aside. Add the tofu cubes to a ziplock bag and pour in the marinade. Seal the bag, and then turn it over a few times to coat the tofu in the marinade. Let the tofu sit for 10 to 15 minutes while you prep the salad ingredients.

Add the lettuce, bell pepper, carrots, cabbage and cilantro to a large bowl. Toss everything together and set aside.

With a slotted spoon, transfer the tofu to the prepared sheet pan. Spread the cubes out and bake for 20 to 25 minutes, until the edges are crispy and darker in color. Flipping halfway through the baking process is optional. Let the tofu cool completely after baking.

(continued)

FOR THE DRESSING

¼ cup (60 g) peanut or nut butter of your choice

2 tbsp (30 ml) soy sauce

2 tbsp (30 ml) rice vinegar

2 tbsp (30 ml) agave or honey, plus more to taste

2 tbsp (30 ml) lime juice (about ½ a lime)

1 tbsp (15 ml) vegetable oil

1 tbsp (15 ml) sesame oil

1-inch (2.5-cm) piece ginger, minced

1 clove garlic, minced

TOPPINGS

1 cup (146 g) peanuts, crushed

1 lime, cut into wedges

Meanwhile, make the dressing. In the same measuring glass you used before, add the peanut butter, soy sauce, rice vinegar, agave, lime juice, vegetable oil, sesame oil, ginger and garlic, and stir well. Taste and adjust flavors to your preference.

Divide the lettuce mixture among three meal prep containers. When the tofu is cool, divide the tofu among the containers on top of the salad. Divide the crushed peanuts among the containers and sprinkle them on top. Add a lime wedge to each container. Transfer the dressing to a container or jar. Seal and store in the fridge.

Storage, Serving and Reheating Notes: This salad can last in the fridge for up to 4 days. It's not freezer friendly and is best served cold or room temperature. Right before eating, add the dressing and a squeeze of lime juice to the salad.

Jerk Shrimp, Corn & Black Bean Salad

Shrimp is the star of this easy chopped salad! Plus, it's the only thing you have to cook, making it a fast and easy recipe to prepare on a Sunday before your workweek starts. It goes really well with the Creamy Avocado Herb Sauce (page 160), or you can just throw a few fresh slices of avocado on top and use your favorite dressing. This salad can easily be repurposed into a wrap, tacos or even nachos for a quick dinner!

Prep Time: 10 minutes | Cook Time: 15 minutes | Servings: 3

FOR THE SHRIMP

1 tsp garlic powder

1 tsp sugar

1 tsp salt

½ tsp paprika

½ tsp ground thyme

½ tsp allspice

½ tsp ground pepper

½ tsp cinnamon

¼ tsp cayenne

1 lb (454 g) shrimp, peeled and deveined

2 tbsp (30 ml) vegetable oil

FOR THE SALAD

1 red bell pepper, chopped small

1 cup (136 g) canned corn or thawed frozen corn

1 cup (172 g) black beans, rinsed and drained

4 radishes, sliced

3 scallions, green ends chopped, white ends discarded

Salt and pepper to taste

1 (9-oz [255-g]) bag of lettuce or romaine (about 8 cups)

1 recipe Quick Pickled Red Onions (page 168)

1 lime, chopped into wedges

1 recipe Creamy Avocado Herb Sauce (page 160)

In a large bowl, mix the garlic powder, sugar, salt, paprika, ground thyme, allspice, ground pepper, cinnamon and cayenne and mix well. Add the prepared shrimp and gently toss to coat it in the spice mix.

Preheat a nonstick or cast-iron skillet on the stove over medium heat for a minute or two, then add the vegetable oil and let it warm up. Add the shrimp and let it cook for 3 to 4 minutes on each side over medium heat, until it's bright pink and has curled up. You may need to cook the shrimp in batches to avoid crowding the pan. Remove the shrimp from the pan and let them cool while you prepare the salad.

In a large bowl, mix the bell pepper, corn, black beans, radishes and scallions and salt and pepper to taste. Toss the ingredients together and set aside.

Divide the lettuce among three large meal prep containers. Top with the bell pepper mixture and cooked shrimp. If using Quick Pickled Red Onions, add them on top. Add a lime wedge to each container. If using the Creamy Avocado Herb Sauce, keep it on the side in three small dressing containers.

Storage, Reheating and Serving Notes: This meal lasts for up to 4 days in the fridge. It's not freezer friendly. I recommend enjoying this meal cold or at room temperature. If you wish, you can heat up the shrimp for this salad. Squeeze the lime wedge, drizzle the dressing on top of the salad and mix with a fork before eating.

Crunchy Mandarin Salad with Salmon

Need a non-lettuce salad? The broccoli slaw base in this recipe makes an ideal salad. It's easy to find, comes pre-chopped and it's delicious! You can swap salmon out for any protein you'd like in this salad recipe. Want to turn this salad into a stir-fry? Just add rice or noodles.

Prep Time: 15 minutes | Cook Time: 20 minutes | Servings: 3

FOR THE SALMON

1 lb (454 g) salmon

2 tbsp (30 ml) honey

3 cloves garlic, minced

1-inch (2.5-cm) piece ginger, minced

1 tbsp (15 ml) rice vinegar

2 tsp (10 ml) sriracha

2 tsp (10 ml) sesame oil

1 tbsp (15 ml) soy sauce

1 mandarin, halved

Cooking spray

SALAD INGREDIENTS

1 [12-oz (336-g)] bag of broccoli slaw

3 mandarins, peeled and separated into slices

8 radishes, sliced

1 cup (119 g) edamame, cooked according to the package

⅔ cup (11 g) chopped cilantro

½ cup (80 g) cashews or almonds, chopped

1 cup (56 g) fried chow mein noodles, for topping, optional

SESAME MANDARIN DRESSING

½ cup (120 ml) toasted sesame oil

2 tbsp (30 ml) soy sauce

¼ cup (60 ml) honey

2 tsp (10 ml) rice vinegar

3 tbsp (27 g) sesame seeds

2 mandarins, halved

Preheat your oven to 400°F (200°C). Cut the salmon into three pieces.

To a measuring glass, add the honey, garlic, ginger, rice vinegar, sriracha, sesame oil and soy sauce. Squeeze juice from the two mandarin halves over the glass and mix well. Prepare a baking sheet or dish with cooking spray. Place the salmon on the dish and pour the glaze on top. Use a spoon to scoop up sauce from the bottom of the dish and drizzle it on the salmon, ensuring the tops and sides of the fillets are completely covered in the sauce. Bake for 15 to 20 minutes, until the salmon is firm to the touch or a meat thermometer reads 140°F (60°C). If more caramelization is desired, broil the salmon for exactly 1 minute before taking it out of the oven.

While the salmon bakes, toss the broccoli slaw, mandarin slices, radishes, cooked edamame, cilantro and cashews. Set aside.

To make the dressing, add the sesame oil, soy sauce, honey, rice vinegar and sesame seeds to the same measuring glass you used before. Add the juice of two mandarins and mix. Transfer the dressing to small containers to keep on the side until you eat the salad.

Divide the broccoli slaw mixture among three meal prep containers. Place the cooked salmon on top.

Storage, Reheating and Serving Notes: This meal lasts for 3 to 4 days in the fridge. It's not freezer friendly. Enjoy this meal cold or at room temperature. You can reheat the salmon in the microwave, on the stove or in the oven if you'd like! The salmon should flake apart easily when you're ready to eat. Drizzle the dressing on top before eating.

Loaded Kale Chicken Caesar Salad

I've been known to grab a takeout Caesar salad in a crunch during a workday, but none have ever come close to how good this recipe tastes. Kale holds up way better than lettuce in most cases, making this salad easy to store in the fridge or quickly assemble. You can swap some ingredients for pre-made ones, like rotisserie chicken or store-bought dressing to save time.

Prep Time: 15 minutes | Cook Time: 20 minutes | Servings: 3

FOR THE CHICKEN

3 tbsp (45 ml) olive oil, divided

1 tsp oregano

1 tsp garlic powder

½ tsp salt

½ tsp ground pepper

¼ tsp crushed red pepper

1 lb (454 g) chicken breast

FOR THE DRESSING

3 oil-packed anchovies, chopped

1 clove garlic, minced

¾ tsp salt

½ tsp ground pepper

1 tsp Dijon mustard

½ tsp Worcestershire sauce

⅓ cup (80 ml) mayonnaise

¼ cup (25 g) Parmesan cheese

FOR THE SALAD

3 eggs, for boiling, optional

3 cups (200 g) kale, chopped

A pinch of salt

½ cup (50 g) Parmesan cheese

2 cups (112 g) croutons, optional

1 avocado, for topping, optional

Preheat your oven to 425° F (220° C). Add 2 tablespoons (30 ml) of olive oil to a measuring glass with the oregano, garlic powder, salt, pepper and crushed red pepper. Place the chicken breast in a baking dish and pour the olive oil mixture on top. Use your hands or a spoon to rub the oil and spices on both sides of the chicken. Bake for 15 to 17 minutes, or until the chicken is firm to the touch and a meat thermometer reads 165°F (74°C). When it's finished cooking, let the chicken rest for at least 15 minutes.

Meanwhile, make the dressing. Add the anchovies, garlic, salt, pepper, Dijon mustard, Worcestershire, mayonnaise and ¼ cup (25 g) of the Parmesan cheese to a food processor. Process until smooth and well blended. Taste the dressing to adjust the seasonings, and then transfer it to a small container or jar. The dressing will last for about 10 days in the fridge.

If using eggs, bring a pot of water to boil, using enough water to fully cover 3 eggs when submerged. Once the water is boiling, place the eggs gently in the water with a spoon. Reduce the heat slightly and cover the pot. Let the eggs cook for 6 minutes if you'd like a soft egg, 8 minutes for a medium egg and 10 minutes for a hard-boiled egg. Prepare a bowl with cold or ice water while the eggs cook. When they're done, transfer them carefully to the cold water and let them cool. You can store them unpeeled for up to 5 days in the fridge.

Place the kale in a large bowl. Add the remaining 1 tablespoon (15 ml) of olive oil to the bowl with a pinch or two of salt. Gently toss and massage the kale until it becomes soft and bright green in color. When the chicken has cooled, slice it into strips against the grain with a sharp knife. Then chop those strips into bite-sized cubes. Store the kale, chicken, eggs, dressing and cheese separately and assemble before you eat or head to work.

Storage, Reheating and Serving Notes: This meal lasts for up to 4 days in the fridge. It's not freezer friendly. I recommend eating this salad cold or at room temperature!

My Favorite Spinach Greek Salad

Greek salads are one of the first meal preps I tried to make when I first started prepping lunches! I used to buy one almost every day for a while at a fast-casual spot in NYC called Cosi, but making them myself saved so much money. The trick to nailing this salad is swapping tomatoes for red bell pepper. Red bell peppers hold up way better in meal preps and they add a nice crunch! You can enjoy this salad stuffed into a pita for a more filling meal instead of just eating a few pita slices on the side.

Prep Time: 15 minutes | Cook Time: 15 minutes | Servings: 3

FOR THE CHICKEN

1 lb (454 g) chicken breast, sliced into thin cutlets

1 tbsp (6 g) za'atar

¾ tsp salt

½ tsp ground pepper

1 tbsp (15 ml) olive oil

FOR THE SALAD

3 cups (100 g) spinach, roughly chopped

1 small red bell pepper, chopped

1 small green bell pepper, chopped

⅔ cup (109 g) olives, sliced

½ cup (62 g) chopped red onion

1 cup (28 g) chopped parsley

1 cup (150 g) feta cheese

3 pitas, for serving

FOR THE DRESSING

¼ cup (80 ml) honey

¼ cup (80 ml) Dijon mustard

¼ cup (80 ml) olive oil

1 tbsp (15 ml) apple cider vinegar

1 tbsp (15 ml) water

1 tbsp (15 ml) lemon juice

Salt and pepper to taste

¼ tsp crushed red pepper flakes, optional

Preheat a cast-iron skillet over medium heat for a few minutes. Meanwhile, pat the chicken dry and sprinkle both sides with the za'atar, salt and pepper. Add the olive oil to the cast-iron skillet, and after a minute add the seasoned chicken breast. Cook on each side for 5 to 7 minutes, until the chicken is golden in color, firm to the touch and reads 160°F (71°C) on a meat thermometer, if you have one. Let the chicken rest while you prepare the salad.

Get three large meal prep containers ready. Divide the spinach among the three of them, followed by the red and green bell pepper, olives, red onion, parsley and feta. You can mix the ingredients together before you eat, but for meal prep purposes it's best to keep them separated in the container. If making dressing, prepare it and keep it in a container on the side. Keep the pita bread on the side as well.

To make the dressing, add the honey, Dijon mustard, olive oil, apple cider vinegar, water, lemon juice, salt and pepper to taste and crushed red pepper flakes, if desired. Use a fork to stir the ingredients until smooth and combined. Taste and adjust the flavors to your preferences. Store the dressing in three small containers on the side.

Once the chicken has cooled, slice it into strips and place on top of the veggies in the containers.

Storage, Reheating and Serving Notes: This salad lasts for up to 4 days in the fridge and tastes great cold or room temperature! Enjoy with pita bread on the side.

BETTER THAN TAKEOUT

I wouldn't be where I am today if takeout meals hadn't inspired me so much.

My go-to fast-casual lunch spot was Dig Inn, where I'd get a plate with a protein, some vegetables and a grain for $13 a pop. My usual was a huge plate with salmon, sweet potatoes and kale, which always left me feeling so stuffed in the afternoon. One weekend I decided I wanted to make my own, even though I had never cooked a sweet potato before, let alone salmon. Turns out, you can make three of that same meal at home for the cost of one at Dig Inn! I never looked back. Find my sheet-pan salmon recipe on page 36.

As my cooking repertoire grew, I looked to other popular takeout dishes to try at home with my own spin, like my Ramen Chicken Pad Thai (page 105). It's not just that I enjoy the savings of making takeout meals at home to eat at work, it's also learning the cooking skills required to make these taste just as good, if not better.

The best containers for these meals will be your standard glass or plastic 30-oz (887-ml) ones. The ramen recipe (page 106) is a little more complicated to store, especially if you're making the soy-marinated eggs, but I promise it's worth it. You'll need some two-compartment containers and mason jars for that one.

If making your own Indian-inspired takeout meals, like Tofu Tikka Masala (page 109) or Kimchi Veggie Fried Rice (page 96), intimidates you, you're not alone. I always thought I'd need top chef level skills to master them, or I'd have to scour international supermarkets for the right ingredients. The good news is that you can make your favorite takeout meals with affordable, easy to-find ingredients and basic cooking skills you probably already have!

Another aspect to these meals is their flexibility. You can generally swap any of these veggies out for ones you specifically enjoy or what's in season near you, especially in dishes like My Go-To Teriyaki Chicken & Veggies recipe (page 102). But I wouldn't change too much about these sauces! I promise you'll use these shelf-stable ingredients over and over again once you try these takeout-inspired meals.

Meal prep works best when you make meals you know you'll look forward to eating during the day or after work. If you love takeout as much as me, it's time to start learning how to make your favorite dishes at home so you don't have to deal with all the delivery fees or long lines during the workday.

Kimchi Veggie Fried Rice

I always look forward to fried rice at work. It's comforting, delicious and keeps me energized throughout the afternoon. The star of this veggie-forward fried rice is kimchi! You can generally find kimchi in the grocery store with the tofu, or sometimes near the produce. Traditionally, kimchi fried rice is topped with a fried egg, but boiled eggs are easier to meal prep!

Prep Time: 10 minutes | Cook Time: 35 minutes | Servings: 3

FOR THE RICE AND SOFT-BOILED EGGS

¾ cup (150 g) rice

1½ cups (360 ml) water

½ tsp salt

3 eggs

FOR THE SAUCE

3 tbsp (45 ml) soy sauce

2 tbsp (30 ml) kimchi liquid from the jar

1 tbsp (15 ml) chili garlic sauce or gochujang

2 tsp (10 ml) sriracha, optional

1 tsp sugar

2 tsp (10 ml) sesame oil

FOR EVERYTHING ELSE

2 tbsp (30 ml) olive oil, divided

2 eggs

To a pot, add the rice, water and salt. Bring it to a boil, then cover and reduce to a simmer. Let the rice simmer for 10 minutes, then turn off the heat and let it steam for 10 minutes. When the rice is fully cooked, fluff it with a fork and pour it onto a large plate or sheet pan so it can dry out a bit.

For the eggs, fill another pot with enough water to submerge your eggs. Bring the water to a boil, then carefully place the eggs in the pot. Bring the heat down to medium and cover the pot. For a soft egg, cook the eggs for 7 minutes. Meanwhile, fill a medium-sized bowl with cold water and stick it in the fridge. When the 7 minutes is up, transfer the eggs to the cold water and let them cool completely. Don't peel these until you're ready to eat.

For the sauce, add the soy sauce, kimchi liquid, chili garlic sauce, sriracha, if using, sugar and sesame oil in a measuring glass. Stir well until combined and set aside.

(continued)

Kimchi Veggie Fried Rice (continued)

½ cup (80 g) chopped yellow onion (about ½ an onion)

2 cloves garlic, minced

3 scallions, white and green ends chopped and separated, roots discarded

Salt and pepper to taste

1 cup (170 g) kimchi, chopped

1 cup (75 g) chopped red cabbage

2 cups (226 g) shiitake mushrooms, chopped

2 cups (166 g) snap peas

Heat up the largest nonstick skillet or pan you have. Add half of the olive oil and let it warm up. Crack the eggs into the pan and scramble over medium heat. While scrambling, add 1 to 2 teaspoons (5 to 10 ml) of the prepared sauce. When the eggs are firm and cooked through, remove them from the pan, but keep the heat on.

Add the remaining olive oil to the pan over medium heat. After a minute, add the onion, garlic and white ends of the scallions. Add salt and pepper to taste. Cook, stirring often, for 5 to 7 minutes until the onion has softened. Add the kimchi, cabbage, mushrooms and snap peas. Cook over high heat, stirring often for about 10 minutes, until the cabbage and snap peas are fork-tender.

Add the green ends of the scallions, scrambled egg and cooked rice to the skillet. Pour in the sauce and stir everything together. Cook for an additional 5 to 7 minutes over high heat, stirring often.

Divide the fried rice among three meal prep containers. Garnish with extra scallions if you have any left. Leave the soft-boiled egg on the side until you eat!

Storage, Reheating and Serving Notes: This fried rice can last in the fridge for up to 5 days. Peel the soft-boiled eggs before you eat. You can reheat it on the stove or in the microwave. It's also good at room temperature. Halfway through reheating, add the soft-boiled egg on top to warm it up without cooking it too much more.

Sticky Bourbon Chicken & Rice

Confession: I cook more with spirits than I drink them! This bourbon chicken is inspired by the sticky sweet chicken dishes you'd find in mall food courts, but it's so much tastier and is perfect for lunch. While you're cooking the chicken, you can cook the vegetables and rice in one go. This is one of my favorite meal prep hacks to speed up cooking time while covering all the bases.

Prep Time: 10 minutes | Cook Time: 40 minutes | Servings: 3

FOR THE CHICKEN

2 tbsp (16 g) cornstarch

½ tsp salt

¼ tsp ground pepper

1 lb (454 g) chicken breast, chopped into chunks

¼ cup (60 ml) vegetable oil

FOR THE VEGGIE RICE

1 tsp olive oil

1 large carrot, peeled and chopped

1 red bell pepper, chopped

1 cup (134 g) frozen peas

Pinch of salt

¾ cup (150 g) rice

1½ cups (360 ml) water

2 scallions, green ends chopped, for garnish, optional

For the chicken, add the cornstarch to a big bowl with salt and pepper, and mix. Add the chicken to the bowl and toss the chicken to coat it in the cornstarch.

Heat up a skillet for 2 to 3 minutes over medium heat. Then add the vegetable oil and let it heat up for two minutes, until very hot. Using tongs, carefully add the chicken to the pan. It helps to tilt the pan away from you as you do this. You may need to cook the chicken in two batches to avoid overcrowding the pan. Cook on each side for 5 minutes—it should be golden and crispy. When cooked through, set the chicken aside.

For the rice, add the olive oil to a pot over medium-high heat. Add in the carrot, bell pepper and peas with a pinch of salt, and then cook, stirring frequently, on high heat for a minute. Add in the rice and water. Bring the pot to a boil, then reduce to a simmer and cover with a tight-fitting lid. Cook over low heat for 10 minutes, then turn off the heat to let the rice steam.

(continued)

FOR THE SAUCE

½ cup (120 ml) water

⅓ cup (80 ml) soy sauce

¼ cup (60 ml) bourbon (sub maple syrup) with 1 tbsp (15 ml) vanilla extract

¼ cup (60 ml) orange or apple juice

¼ cup (60 ml) chicken broth

2 tbsp (30 ml) ketchup

1 tbsp (15 ml) apple cider vinegar

⅓ cup (73 g) brown sugar

½ tsp onion powder

¼ tsp crushed red pepper

1 clove garlic, minced

2 tsp (10 ml) sriracha, optional

For the sauce, add the water, soy sauce, bourbon with vanilla extract, orange juice, chicken broth, ketchup, apple cider vinegar, brown sugar, onion powder, crushed red pepper and minced garlic to a measuring glass or bowl. Whisk well until all the ingredients are combined. Add in the sriracha if you want an extra kick. Make sure to taste it and adjust the flavors to your preference before adding the sauce to the chicken.

Heat the same pan you used for the chicken over medium heat. Pour in the sauce and bring it to a boil. Add the chicken back to the sauce, turn down the heat to low and let the sauce cook uncovered for 8 to 10 minutes, until it's reduced by about half, stirring occasionally. The heat should be high enough so the sauce bubbles gently.

Divide the cooked chicken and rice among three meal prep containers. Garnish with scallions if desired. Let the meals cool for at least 20 minutes before covering them and storing them in the fridge.

Storage, Reheating and Serving Notes: This takeout-inspired dish can last in the fridge for up to 4 days and is not freezer friendly. You can reheat it in the microwave or on the stove.

My Go-To Teriyaki Chicken & Veggies

The method for this delicious teriyaki chicken recipe is based on what I learned from a chef in Japan. This is an easy, straightforward meal with tons of flavor that you'll look forward to no matter what you have going on at work.

Prep Time: 10 minutes | Cook Time: 30 minutes | Servings: 3

FOR THE CHICKEN

1 tbsp (15 ml) cooking sake or rice vinegar

¾ cup (180 ml) water

1 tsp salt

1 lb (454 g) chicken thighs or breast

¼ cup (60 ml) vegetable oil for cooking the chicken

FOR THE RICE

¾ cup (150 g) rice

1½ cups (360 ml) water

Pinch of salt

TERIYAKI SAUCE

3 tbsp (45 ml) soy sauce

2 tbsp (30 ml) mirin

2 tbsp (30 ml) honey

½ tsp salt

3 tbsp (45 ml) cooking sake or 1 tbsp (15 ml) rice vinegar

⅓ cup (80 ml) water

2 cloves garlic

1-inch (2.5-cm) piece ginger, minced

VEGETABLES

1 tbsp (15 ml) olive oil

1 large head of broccoli, chopped into florets

3 carrots, peeled and chopped into ½-inch (1.3-cm) thick rounds

1 tbsp (15 ml) soy sauce

To marinate the chicken, mix the cooking sake, water and salt in a bowl or ziplock bag. Add the chicken thighs to the bag and gently toss to coat. Set aside for 30 minutes.

For the rice, add the rice to a pot with the water and a pinch of salt. Bring to a boil, then reduce to a simmer, cover and cook for 10 minutes on low heat. Then turn the heat off and let the rice steam for another 10 minutes. Fluff with a fork, then keep covered until you're ready to assemble.

For the sauce, add the soy sauce, mirin, honey, salt, cooking sake, water, garlic and ginger to a measuring glass. Taste the mixture. If you want it to be sweeter, add more honey. If you want it to be saltier, add more soy sauce.

Remove the chicken from the marinade and pat it dry with a paper towel. Heat up a nonstick skillet over medium heat for 2 minutes, then add the vegetable oil and let it heat up for 2 minutes, until it's very hot. Carefully add the chicken to the pan, smoother side down, and cook for 4 to 5 minutes over medium-high heat. I wouldn't put more than four pieces in at a time to avoid overcrowding. Flip and repeat. When the chicken has color on both sides, turn down the heat to low. Add the sauce to the pan. If cooking in batches, add half the sauce. Let the sauce simmer and thicken for about 5 minutes, flipping the chicken periodically to coat it in the sauce. Repeat this process if cooking in batches. Set the chicken aside when it's done and let it rest. Feel free to brush the chicken with extra sauce from the pan.

Wipe the pan out if needed, then return it to the stove. Add the olive oil, broccoli and carrots with the soy sauce. Stir-fry over medium-high heat for 7 to 8 minutes, until the veggies are tender-crisp. Cut the chicken into strips. Divide the rice among three containers, followed by the veggies and chicken.

Storage, Reheating and Serving Notes: This meal can last in the fridge for up to 4 days. It's not freezer friendly. Reheat in the microwave or on the stove, or enjoy room temperature!

Ramen Chicken Pad Thai

Pad Thai is traditionally made with rice noodles, but ramen noodles add a nice twist. Plus, they're easier and faster to cook. Pad Thai is a go-to for takeout, but I like making it at home so I can add as many vegetables as I want!

Prep Time: 15 minutes | Cook Time: 30 minutes | Servings: 3

FOR THE SAUCE

2 tbsp (30 ml) ketchup

3 tbsp (42 g) brown sugar

3 tbsp (45 ml) fish sauce

2 tbsp (30 ml) rice vinegar

1 tbsp (15 ml) oyster sauce

2 tsp (10 ml) soy sauce

FOR EVERYTHING ELSE

2½ tbsp (37 ml) vegetable oil, divided

1 lb (454 g) chicken, chopped into thin strips and patted dry

½ tsp salt

2 eggs, whisked

2 carrots, peeled and chopped into matchsticks

1 zucchini, chopped into matchsticks

3–4 scallions, white and green ends separated, chopped

1 tbsp (15 ml) soy sauce

2 (3-oz [85-g]) packages of ramen noodles, flavor packet discarded

2 limes, 1 halved, 1 cut into wedges

¾ cup (12 g) chopped cilantro, optional

½ cup (73 g) peanuts, crushed

Add the ketchup, brown sugar, fish sauce, rice vinegar, oyster sauce and soy sauce to a measuring glass. Stir well to combine and set aside. Bring a pot of water to boil for the ramen just to have it ready.

Heat up a large skillet over medium heat for 3 to 5 minutes. Add half of the vegetable oil and let it heat up for 2 to 3 minutes. Add the chicken to the pan and season it with the salt. Cook the chicken on each side for 3 to 4 minutes over medium heat, or until you have a good sear on the pieces and it's completely cooked through. Remove the chicken from the pan and set aside.

Add ½ tablespoon (7.5 ml) of oil to the skillet and pour in the eggs. Scramble over medium heat until the eggs are fully cooked through, for about 3 minutes. Remove the cooked eggs from the pan and set aside.

Add the remaining vegetable oil to the skillet over medium heat. Then add the carrots, zucchini and white ends of the scallions. Add 1 table-spoon (15 ml) of soy sauce. Cook for 5 to 7 minutes over medium heat, until the veggies are tender-crisp. Add the chicken and egg back to the skillet.

Place the ramen noodles in the boiling water and cook them according to the package directions. They generally cook in 3 to 4 minutes. Drain the noodles when they're cooked and add them to the skillet with the other cooked ingredients. Add the sauce to the pan and use tongs to mix everything together over medium heat for 2 to 3 minutes. Turn off the heat and squeeze the juice of two lime halves over the pot.

Divide the ramen pad Thai among three meal prep containers. Top with cilantro (if using), peanuts and lime wedges.

Storage, Reheating and Serving Notes: This noodle dish can last in the fridge for up to 4 days. It's not freezer friendly. If reheating using the microwave, partially cover the container to moisten the noodles.

Coconut Curry Ramen

Yes! You can meal prep ramen! It's way more meal prep friendly than you'd think. In this recipe, we're storing the noodles, fillings, broth and marinated soft-boiled egg separately. All you have to do is heat the broth, the fillings and the optional egg and you've got meal prep ramen! Throw on your favorite toppings and enjoy. I love sriracha and garlic on mine. This is not a traditional ramen, as we're using roasted vegetables, but the flavors are incredible.

Prep Time: 10 minutes | Cook Time: 45 minutes | Servings: 3

2 cups (255 g) chopped eggplant (about ½ a large eggplant)

3 tbsp (45 ml) olive oil

1½ tsp (4 g) salt, divided

1 tsp ground pepper, divided

2 cups (226 g) baby bella mushrooms, sliced

1 tbsp (15 ml) vegetable oil

1-inch (2.5-cm) piece ginger, minced

2 cloves garlic, minced

2–3 scallions, white and green ends sliced and separated

1 tbsp (18 g) miso paste

2 tbsp (12 g) red curry paste

1 tsp curry powder

4 cups (960 ml) vegetable broth

2 cups (480 ml) water

2 tbsp (30 ml) soy sauce

1 (15-oz [420-ml]) can coconut milk

2 (3-oz [85-g]) packages ramen noodles, flavor packets discarded

1 lime, cut into wedges, for garnish, optional

Preheat the oven to 400°F (200°C). Toss the eggplant in a bowl with 1½ tablespoons (23 ml) of olive oil, salt and pepper. Pour the eggplant onto a sheet pan and bake for 25 to 30 minutes, flipping halfway. If the eggplant looks dry when you flip, add a drizzle of oil before placing back in the oven. When finished, the eggplant should be very soft, have a sweet flavor and have color around the edges. If it tastes bitter, it needs more time in the oven.

In a large Dutch oven or large pot over medium heat, add the remaining 1½ tablespoons (23 ml) of olive oil. After a minute, add the mushrooms with salt and pepper. Sauté for 10 to 15 minutes over medium heat, until the mushrooms have darkened in color and have cooked down in size. Remove them and set them aside.

In the same Dutch oven or pot over medium heat, add the vegetable oil, ginger, garlic, white ends of the scallions, miso paste and red curry paste. Stir the mixture constantly for a few minutes, until fragrant. If the pot looks dry in the process, add a splash of water. Add the curry powder, vegetable broth, water, soy sauce and coconut milk to the pot and let the mixture simmer for 5 to 10 minutes.

With the mixture still simmering, add the ramen and let it cook through according to the time on the package, usually around 5 minutes.

When the ramen is cooked through, strain the broth over a bowl or another pot to separate the noodles and broth. Store the noodles in a container with a little water to keep them soft. When the broth cools, transfer it to a large jar. Store the cooked eggplant, mushrooms and green ends of the scallions in another container.

(continued)

Coconut Curry Ramen (continued)

FOR THE MARINATED EGGS (OPTIONAL)

3 eggs
½ cup (120 ml) soy sauce
¼ cup (60 ml) water
½ cup (120 ml) mirin

For the soft-boiled marinated eggs, boil 4 to 5 cups (946 ml to 1.2 L) of water in a pot. When the water is boiling, add the eggs, turn the heat down to medium and cover the pot. Set a timer for 6 to 7 minutes for a soft-boiled egg. For medium eggs, set the timer for 9 to 11 minutes, and for hard-boiled eggs, set the timer for 12 to 14 minutes. Meanwhile, prepare a bowl of cold water with ice and place it in the fridge—if you don't have ice, this still works. When the eggs are done cooking, transfer them carefully to the bowl of cold water and let them cool completely. Meanwhile, mix the soy sauce, water and mirin in a container. When the eggs have cooled, you can peel them and place them in the marinade for up to 24 hours, and then drain the marinade and keep them in the fridge for up to 4 days.

To assemble this meal, place one-third of the cooked noodles, one-third of the eggplant and mushroom and the scallions in a bowl. Fill it with the broth. Heat this up in the microwave or on the stove. Meanwhile, cut one of your marinated eggs in half. When ready to eat, place the eggs on top and squeeze some lime over the ramen. Enjoy!

Storage, Reheating and Serving Notes: This meal can last in the fridge for up to 4 days. It's not freezer friendly. I don't recommend storing ramen mixed together! The assembly takes a bit more time, but it's worth it.

Tofu Tikka Masala

My coworkers at my last job before starting Workweek Lunch used to love grabbing Indian takeout at lunch time. It smelled so good, but I always preferred bringing my own rather than waiting in those long lines during the lunch rush hour. This recipe uses tofu instead of chickpeas, which you traditionally see in a vegetarian tikka masala recipe, because tofu has a lovely texture in the creamy sauce over fluffy rice!

Prep Time: 10 minutes | Cook Time: 45 minutes | Servings: 3

FOR THE TOFU

1 (14-oz [392-ml]) package of firm tofu, drained and pressed for 10 minutes

Cooking spray

2 tbsp (30 ml) soy sauce

2 tbsp (30 ml) water

2 tsp (10 ml) red curry paste

1 tsp honey or agave

1 tsp garam masala

2 tbsp (30 ml) olive oil

Preheat the oven to 400°F (200°C) while your tofu presses for 10 to 30 minutes.

Prepare a baking sheet with cooking spray. Add the soy sauce, water, red curry paste, honey, garam masala and olive oil to a measuring glass and mix well. Chop the tofu into cubes and place them in a zip-lock bag or mixing bowl. Pour the soy sauce mixture over the tofu and gently toss to coat. Let it sit for 15 minutes, then pour the tofu onto the baking sheet. Bake for 20 to 30 minutes, flipping halfway, until the tofu is crispy around the edges.

(continued)

Tofu Tikka Masala (continued)

1 tbsp (15 ml) olive oil

½ onion, chopped

3 cloves of garlic, minced

1-inch (2.5-cm) piece ginger, minced

2 tsp (6 g) garam masala

2 tsp (6 g) cumin

1 tsp salt, divided

½ head of cauliflower, chopped into florets

1 (28-oz [784-ml]) can crushed tomatoes

2 tsp (6 g) chili powder

¾ cup (150 g) rice

1½ cups (360 ml) water

1 tsp olive oil or butter

½ cup (120 ml) heavy cream

1 tsp brown sugar

1 bunch of cilantro, chopped, stems discarded

1 lime, cut into wedges

3–4 pieces of naan, for serving, optional

Heat up a large skillet or Dutch oven over medium heat, and then add the olive oil. After a minute, add the onion, garlic, ginger, garam masala, cumin and half of the salt. Sauté, stirring frequently, for about 5 minutes. Add the cauliflower florets to the pan and stir to coat the cauliflower in the spice mixture. Add the crushed tomatoes and chili powder to the cauliflower mixture, and stir well. Cover and let the mixture simmer for 10 to 15 minutes.

Meanwhile, to a medium-sized pot, add the rice and water with the olive oil and remaining salt. Bring the pot to a boil, then cover it with a lid and reduce the heat to a simmer. Let it cook for 10 minutes, and then turn off the heat and let the rice steam for 10 minutes before fluffing with a fork.

To the tomato mixture, add the heavy cream, brown sugar and half of the cilantro. At this point, taste the mixture to adjust the seasoning as necessary. Finally, add the tofu and stir gently to coat it in the sauce.

Divide the tikka masala and rice among three containers. Top with extra cilantro and a lime wedge. Keep naan, if using, on the side. If you have leftover tikka masala, it can be frozen!

Storage, Reheating and Serving Notes: Tofu Tikka Masala can last in the fridge for up to 5 days and is freezer friendly. You can reheat it in the microwave or on the stove. Make sure to remove the lime wedge and cover the container loosely if microwaving so the rice steams a bit. Squeeze the lime wedge over the meal before eating and enjoy with naan!

THE FREEZER STASH

Here's a secret. You don't have to cook every weekend to reap the benefits of meal prep if you build up a freezer stash of lunches! All of these meals are freezer friendly and easy to thaw and reheat. Ideally, these are the meals you'll pull out for work lunches after a vacation. No one wants to spend hours in the kitchen after a flight or weekend getaway! Your freezer stash is here for those situations. It's also great to build up a stash for times when you might feel under the weather.

Soups, chilis, stews and casseroles are ideal freezer meal preps because they don't require any attention when reheating. You can simply pop them in the microwave still frozen or let them thaw in the fridge. These types of meals still taste great after you reheat them after being frozen. When you load up the toppings on our Cozy Chicken Tortilla Soup (page 115), you won't even remember you froze it! Of course, these meals are tasty as well, and can last up to 5 days in the fridge.

You can use glass or plastic containers for freezer meals! Just keep in mind that not all glass containers are oven friendly if you choose to reheat meals in the oven. Also, be sure to leave enough space in the container in case the food expands while frozen, which is normal.

These comfort food recipes will also spark a bit of nostalgia! My Veggie Chili Mac 'N' Cheese recipe (page 119) transports me back to childhood camping trips even while I'm sitting at my desk, and the classic chicken noodle soup gets a tangy upgrade with a twist of lemon in my Lemon Chicken & Rice Soup (page 120).

Another thing I love about freezer meals is that you can assemble them, pop them in the freezer and bake them from frozen if you're working from home or want to enjoy one of these for dinner! You can try this method out in the Cheesy Penne Spinach Pesto Bake (page 123), where you'll prep individual lasagnas in glass containers. This also cuts down on mess since you'll eat it directly from the container and skip the whole giant casserole dish part!

Cozy Chicken Tortilla Soup

Whenever I have chicken tortilla soup in my freezer, it always goes so fast. Luckily, it's an easy one-pot meal to make on a weekend while catching up on podcasts. We all know the best part of tortilla soup is the toppings! Load up your bowl of tortilla soup with chips, avocado, cheese, sour cream and cilantro for a cozy, comforting lunch.

Prep Time: 10 minutes | Cook Time: 35 minutes | Servings: 4

1 tbsp (15 ml) olive oil

1 cup (160 g) chopped yellow onion

3 cloves garlic, minced

3 scallions, chopped, white and green ends separated, roots discarded

2–3 chipotle peppers in adobo sauce, chopped and deseeded if desired

2 tsp (10 ml) adobo sauce (from can of peppers)

1 (15-oz [420-ml]) can pinto beans, drained

1 (28-oz [784-ml]) can crushed tomatoes

1 (14-oz [392-ml]) can cream style corn

1 red bell pepper, chopped

3 tsp (8 g) cumin

2 tsp (6 g) chili powder

1 tsp dried oregano

2 cups (480 ml) chicken broth

Salt and pepper to taste

12 oz (336 g) chicken breast, halved if thick

1 cup (113 g) shredded cheese

1 cup (16 g) cilantro, optional

1 avocado, optional

Tortilla chips of your choice

Heat up a large pot or Dutch oven over medium heat. After a few minutes, add the olive oil and let it warm up for a minute or two. Add the onion, garlic and white ends of the scallions. Cook for 3 to 5 minutes, stirring often, until fragrant. Add the chipotle peppers and adobo sauce in the last minute of cooking and stir to incorporate.

To the same pot, add the beans, tomatoes with juices, corn, bell pepper, cumin, chili powder, oregano and chicken broth. Add salt and pepper to taste. Stir well, and then add chicken breasts to the pot. Push them down to submerge them in the broth. Bring the soup to a boil, and then cover and turn the heat down to simmer for 25 to 30 minutes. Stir occasionally, scraping up any bits that stick to the bottom of the pot.

When the chicken is cooked through, remove it from the pot and shred it with two forks on a cutting board. Taste the soup and adjust the seasoning as needed. Add the chicken back in and stir.

Divide into meal prep containers. Let the meals cool for 20 minutes and freeze at this point if desired. If you're eating this meal without freezing it, top each container with cheese, cilantro and the green ends of the scallions. Keep the avocado and tortilla chips on the side until you eat!

Storage, Reheating and Serving Notes: This soup can last in the fridge for up to 5 days and can be frozen for up to 6 months. You can thaw and/or reheat it in the microwave or on the stove. If eating from frozen, top with extra cheese and scallions after reheating. Enjoy with fresh avocado slices and as many of your favorite tortilla chips as you want!

White Bean Chili Verde

This chili is smoky, a little spicy and super satisfying. Instead of using tomatoes and beef like a traditional chili, we're using white beans and tomatillo-based ingredients like green enchilada sauce. The key to getting the right texture in this chili is gently mashing half of the white beans to thicken it up. Don't forget to stir in the sour cream at the end! It takes this dish to the next level.

Prep Time: 10 minutes | Cook Time: 30 minutes | Servings: 4

1 tbsp (15 ml) olive oil

1 cup (160 g) chopped yellow onion

2 (15-oz [420-ml]) cans white beans, divided

3 scallions, white and green ends chopped and separated

3 cloves garlic, minced

1 (15-oz [420-ml]) can green enchilada sauce

1 (10-oz [283-ml]) can of diced tomatoes and green chiles

1 tsp cumin

1 tsp chili powder

½ tsp chipotle powder

Salt and pepper to taste

1 poblano pepper, chopped

1 jalapeño, seeded and chopped

1½ cups (24 g) chopped cilantro, divided

2 tbsp (30 ml) sour cream, plus extra for topping, optional

1 lime, chopped into wedges

Tortilla chips, for serving, optional

1 avocado, for serving, optional

Shredded cheese, for serving, optional

Heat up a Dutch oven or large pot over medium heat. Add the olive oil and let it warm up for a minute, and then add the onion. Sauté the onion for a few minutes, stirring often, until fragrant.

Add a can of white beans to the pot. Using a fork or masher, if you have one, gently mash the white beans until only a few beans remain whole. This helps thicken the chili.

Add the white ends of the scallions, garlic, enchilada sauce, diced tomatoes and green chiles, cumin, chili powder, chipotle powder and salt and pepper to taste. Bring the mixture to a boil, then reduce to a simmer.

Add the remaining white beans, poblano pepper, jalapeño and half of the cilantro. Stir well and taste to adjust the seasonings and flavors as needed. Let the chili simmer for another 10 to 15 minutes. Turn off the heat and stir in the sour cream.

Divide the chili among four meal prep containers. Divide the remaining cilantro and add a lime wedge to each container. If freezing, let them cool for about 30 minutes before sealing and popping them in the freezer. Keep the cheese and avocado on the side until you eat.

Storage, Reheating and Serving Notes: This chili verde can last in the fridge for up to 5 days. It can be frozen for 6 months. I recommend reheating in the microwave or on the stove. You can reheat this meal directly from frozen if you'd like with the same methods. When ready to enjoy, top with tortilla chips, avocado, more sour cream and some cheese if you'd like.

Veggie Chili Mac 'N' Cheese

Full disclosure, this is the easiest mac 'n' cheese I've ever made. Instead of making a roux for a béchamel cheese sauce, the cheese is directly melted into the pot. Plus, you cook the pasta right in the pot with all the other ingredients. It's like magic. And it tastes incredible.

Prep Time: 10 minutes | Cook Time: 25 minutes | Servings: 4

1 tbsp (15 ml) olive oil

1 cup (160 g) chopped yellow onion

2 cloves garlic, minced

1 tsp cumin

1½ tsp (4 g) chili powder

1 (15-oz [420-ml]) can tomato sauce

1 (15-oz [420-ml]) can fire-roasted diced tomatoes

1 (15-oz [420-ml]) canned pinto beans, rinsed and drained

1 cup (136 g) frozen corn, or canned

1 poblano pepper, chopped

Salt and pepper to taste

2 cups (480 ml) vegetable broth (sub water)

2 cups (300 g) macaroni elbows

1¼ cups (120 g) shredded cheddar cheese

3 scallions, chopped, white ends discarded

In a Dutch oven over medium heat, add the olive oil and let it warm up for a minute or two. Then add the chopped onion and sauté for 3 to 5 minutes, until the onion is translucent.

Add the garlic, cumin and chili powder. If the pan looks dry, add a splash of water. Stir and cook for 1 to 2 minutes, then add the tomato sauce, fire-roasted diced tomatoes, pinto beans, corn, chopped poblano pepper and vegetable broth. Add a big pinch of salt and pepper to taste.

Bring the mixture to a boil. Then add the macaroni elbows and cook for 11 to 13 minutes—double check the package of pasta for the best cooking time. When the pasta is cooked through, turn the heat off and add the cheese to the pot. Mix well until the cheese has fully melted and is well incorporated.

Divide the chili mac among four meal prep containers and top with scallions. Let them cool for at least 20 to 30 minutes before storing in the fridge or freezer!

Storage, Reheating and Serving Notes: This recipe lasts in the fridge for up to 4 days and reheats well in the microwave or on the stove. You can freeze this veggie chili mac for up to 6 months! Thaw in the fridge overnight before reheating or reheat in a pot on the stove or in the microwave. I recommend adding a splash of water to the dish when reheating from frozen.

Lemon Chicken & Rice Soup

This cozy one-pot soup is a great option for your freezer stash of quick lunches that are easy to reheat! Rice can be a little tricky in meal prep soup recipes, but all you have to do is add a splash of water when you reheat it. The final result is a thick, hearty soup that warms the soul and gives you something to look forward to on your lunch break.

Prep Time: 10 minutes | Cook Time: 25 minutes | Servings: 4

1 tbsp (15 ml) olive oil

2 carrots, chopped small (about 240 g)

2 celery ribs, chopped small (about 190 g)

1 cup (160 g) chopped yellow onion

2 cloves garlic, minced

1 tsp salt, divided

½ tsp pepper, divided

1 tsp ground mustard

1 tsp ground thyme

2 bay leaves

4 cups (960 ml) chicken stock

1 cup (240 ml) water

1 lb (454 g) chicken breasts or thighs, sliced into thinner pieces if needed

½ cup (100 g) rice

2 cups (66 g) chopped spinach or kale

½ cup (5 g) chopped fresh dill, plus extra for garnish

½ tsp Worcestershire sauce

½ tsp lemon zest

2 tbsp (30 ml) lemon juice

Crusty bread, for serving, optional

Heat up a large pot or Dutch oven over medium heat. After a minute or two, add the olive oil and let that warm up. Then add the carrots, celery, onion and garlic with half of the salt and pepper. Stir often and cook for about 5 minutes until the veggies are fragrant.

Add the ground mustard, thyme, bay leaves, chicken stock and water. Add the remaining salt and pepper. Bring the mixture to a boil, and then add the chicken and the rice.

Simmer until the chicken is completely cooked through, 10 to 15 minutes. A meat thermometer will read 160°F (90°C) when the chicken is done and ready to rest. Remove the chicken from the pot when it's done cooking and let it rest for a few minutes before shredding or chopping. Then return the chicken to the soup.

Turn off the heat and stir in the spinach, dill, Worcestershire sauce, lemon zest and lemon juice. Remove and discard the bay leaves.

Divide the soup among four meal prep containers. Garnish with extra dill if desired before storing. Keep crusty bread on the side until you eat.

Storage, Reheating and Serving Notes: This recipe lasts in the fridge for 4 to 5 days and reheats well in the microwave or on the stove. You may need to add a little water when reheating as the rice will absorb some of the water while this meal is stored in the fridge. It freezes well for up to 6 months.

Cheesy Penne Spinach Pesto Bake

Pasta bakes for work lunches really cater to your inner child. At least it does for me. I love this recipe for its easy spinach-based homemade pesto, a great way to use up extra greens and get more veggies into this meal. If you're vegetarian, I recommend swapping the chicken sausage out for veggie sausage! And you can easily switch up the vegetables and pasta shape depending on what you have on hand. If your pasta sticks together a bit the next day, reheat this meal partially covered and it will taste fresh!

Prep Time: 5 minutes | Cook Time: 35 minutes | Servings: 4

FOR THE PASTA

Cooking spray

8 oz (226 g) penne

1 tbsp (15 ml) olive oil, plus a little extra for the penne

3 chicken sausage links, chopped into rounds

1 head broccoli, chopped into small florets

½ tsp salt

¼ tsp ground pepper

2 cups (298 g) cherry tomatoes, halved

1 (8-oz [226-g]) bag of shredded mozzarella cheese

FOR THE HOMEMADE PESTO

3 cups (66 g) roughly chopped spinach

1½ cups (42 g) chopped basil

½ cup (54 g) almonds or walnuts

½ cup (50 g) Parmesan cheese

2 cloves garlic, whole

¾ cup (180 ml) olive oil

2 tbsp (30 ml) lemon juice

2 tbsp (30 ml) water

½ tsp salt

¼ tsp ground pepper

Preheat your oven to 375°F (190°C) and prepare a 9 x 13–inch (23 x 33–cm) baking dish with cooking spray.

Bring a pot of water to boil. Then add the penne pasta and cook for 8 to 9 minutes, until the pasta is al dente. Drain the pasta and stir in a very small amount of olive oil. Cover the pot with a lid to keep the pasta from sticking while you prepare the pesto.

Heat up a large skillet over medium heat for a minute or two, then add 1 tablespoon (15 ml) of olive oil. Add the chicken sausage and broccoli with the salt and pepper. Cook for about 10 minutes over medium heat, stirring occasionally, until the broccoli has softened and the chicken sausage has darkened in color. Turn off the heat and set aside.

To a food processor, add the spinach, basil, walnuts, Parmesan cheese, garlic, ½ cup (120 ml) of olive oil, lemon juice, water, salt and pepper. Process until smooth. Taste and adjust the seasonings as necessary.

Transfer the cooked pasta, pesto, chicken sausage and broccoli to the baking dish. Add the chopped cherry tomatoes and two-thirds of the mozzarella. Stir everything to combine. Top with the remaining shredded mozzarella and bake, uncovered, for 20 to 25 minutes until the cheese has fully melted and tomatoes are soft.

Let the bake cool, then divide it among four meal prep containers.

Storage, Reheating and Serving Notes: This recipe lasts in the fridge for up to 5 days and reheats well in the microwave, on the stove or in the oven. I recommend reheating this meal loosely covered to help the pasta steam and soften. You can freeze this meal for up to 6 months.

Lentil Butternut Squash Coconut Curry

Curries are my go-to for times I'm feeling too tired to think of a creative meal for lunch. They get better in the fridge overnight as the flavors intensify and blend together, which is a huge plus! It's also really hard to screw up a curry recipe like this, so even if you don't have all the ingredients, it can still work. Just don't skip the coconut milk!

Prep Time: 10 minutes | Cook Time: 50 minutes | Servings: 4

FOR THE CURRY

2 tbsp (30 ml) olive oil

½ cup (80 g) chopped yellow onion (about ½ an onion)

2 cups (226 g) peeled and chopped butternut squash (about ½ a squash)

1 tsp curry powder

½ tsp cinnamon

Salt and pepper to taste

1 tbsp (6 g) red curry paste

1 [15-oz (420-ml)] can fire-roasted crushed tomatoes

1 cup (192 g) dry red or brown lentils

1½ tsp (4 g) garam masala

1½ tsp (4 g) cumin

1 tsp turmeric

2 cups (480 ml) water

1 [15-oz (420-ml)] can coconut milk

1½ cups (24 g) chopped cilantro, divided

1 lime, cut into wedges, optional

FOR THE RICE

1 cup (200 g) rice

1 tsp olive oil

2 cups (480 ml) water

½ tsp salt

Add the olive oil to a large, deep skillet over medium heat. Add the onion, butternut squash, curry powder, cinnamon, salt and pepper to taste. Cook, uncovered, for 5 to 7 minutes, stirring a few times, then add a splash of water to the pan and cover it with a lid. Cook the butternut squash for 10 to 15 minutes, stirring occasionally, until it starts to soften (it's okay if it's not completely soft all the way through).

Add the red curry paste, fire-roasted crushed tomatoes, lentils, garam masala, cumin, turmeric and more salt and pepper to taste. Stir well, then add the water. Bring the pan to a boil, then reduce to a simmer and partially cover. Simmer for 15 to 17 minutes stirring occasionally, until the lentils are soft and cooked to your preference—we love them extremely soft.

Meanwhile, cook the rice. Add the rice, olive oil, water, and salt to a pot over medium heat. Bring the pot to a boil, then cover with a tight-fitting lid and reduce to a simmer. Let the rice cook on the lowest heat for 10 minutes, then turn the heat off and let it steam for at least 10 minutes.

When the lentils have cooked to your preferred level of doneness, turn the heat off and stir in the coconut milk. Taste the curry and adjust the seasonings as needed—you may want to add more salt. Stir in half of the cilantro.

Divide the curry and rice among four meal prep containers and top with the remaining cilantro. If freezing, let cool for 30 minutes before popping the containers into the freezer. Ideally, you can freeze the rice and curry separately if not using containers with a divider. If you're eating this meal this week, add a lime wedge or two to the containers.

Storage, Reheating and Serving Notes: This curry can last in the fridge for up to 5 days and in the freezer for up to 6 months. Reheat in the microwave or on the stove by first covering the rice partially and adding a few drops of water to steam it back to life.

TORTILLAS TO-GO

Tortillas are one of the most versatile meal prep ingredients in the game. Wraps, burritos, tacos and quesadillas are so fun to meal prep, and I'm going to tell you exactly how to make sure your tortillas don't get soggy.

In the Orange-Marinated Steak Fajitas recipe (page 142) and the Buffalo Chicken Tacos recipe (page 141), you'll keep tortillas on the side and assemble the meals at your desk or in the office kitchen before chowing down. I recommend reheating the fillings first and keeping the tortillas on the side, but you totally don't have to. For the other recipes that involve filling the tortillas with delicious combinations of ingredients, you'll only use ingredients I know for a fact will hold up great, like in our Roasted Chickpea, Avocado & Sweet Potato Wraps (page 133).

I recommend using flour tortillas for all of these recipes. You can use corn tortillas for the tacos if you'd like, but flour tortillas hold up best for meal prep. If you're gluten-free, I recommend assembling wraps before eating, as gluten-free tortillas unfortunately tend to not hold as well. Luckily, all the tortilla types work perfectly for meal prep quesadillas, especially for the Black Bean, Spinach & Pesto Quesadillas (page 138) and the Kimchi Mushroom Quesadillas (page 137).

Reheating tortilla meals can be tricky, but I promise it's worth it. My favorite way to reheat tortilla meals is by microwaving them for a minute or two, then sticking them under the broiler for a minute. If I had a toaster oven, I'd use it, but the broiler works fine as long as you keep an eye on your food before it burns! I love this trick especially with the Loaded Chicken & Refried Bean Burritos (page 131) to get the outside crispy and hot. Using a microwave to reheat tortilla meals is totally fine. For best results, I recommend placing a dry paper towel under your quesadilla or wrapping it around your burrito to soak up extra moisture and avoid sogginess.

Egg & Bacon Brunchwrap Supreme

Here's an easy way to enjoy a frittata for lunch on the go! This recipe involves wrapping a frittata, which is a baked egg slice, in a tortilla and grilling it on the stove to seal it up. Then it becomes a handheld lunch that's easy to enjoy outside or wherever you are when hunger strikes.

Prep Time: 15 minutes | Cook Time: 40 minutes | Servings: 3

Cooking spray

8 eggs

¼ cup (60 ml) milk

¾ tsp salt

½ tsp ground pepper

1 cup (149 g) cherry tomatoes, halved

1 jalapeño, seeded and chopped

1 cup (113 g) shredded Monterey jack cheese, plus more for stuffing

1 cup (60 g) chopped cooked bacon

3 large (10-inch [25-cm]) tortillas

Hot sauce, for serving, optional

Preheat your oven to 375°F (190°C). Prepare a glass 9 x 13–inch (23 x 33–cm) baking dish with cooking spray.

To a bowl, add the eggs, milk, salt and pepper. Whisk well. Pour the whisked egg into the baking dish, followed by the cherry tomatoes, jalapeño, cheese and bacon. Stir to make sure the ingredients are distributed evenly throughout the dish.

Bake uncovered for 25 to 30 minutes, until the edges have browned and the center of the baked frittata is firm. If it jiggles at all, it needs more time. The top will look golden in color when it's done.

Let the frittata cool—it will deflate a bit—and slice it down the center longwise, then twice short-ways to get six pieces.

Heat up a nonstick skillet over low heat. Meanwhile, lay a tortilla on a flat surface. Place one of the frittata slices on the tortilla, flat side down. Sprinkle a little cheese on top, then place a second frittata slice on top, flat side facing up. Fold the tortilla around the frittata like an envelope.

Spray the skillet with cooking spray and place the wrapped frittata seam side down on the pan. Let it cook for 3 to 4 minutes on low heat, then flip it to cook on the other side. You may want to use a small plate or flat lid to keep the wrapped frittata pressed down while it cooks.

Remove the wrapped frittata from the pan and repeat the last two steps for the remaining frittata slices. When cool, wrap these Brunchwrap Supremes in foil or plastic wrap and store in the fridge. Keep optional hot sauce and any additonal toppings on the side.

Storage, Reheating and Serving Notes: This recipe can last in the fridge for up to 4 days or frozen for up to 6 months. Reheat it in the microwave for one minute, then sticking it in the oven or toaster oven to crisp back up for a few minutes. You can also reheat it, covered, on the stove. Enjoy with your favorite hot sauce.

Loaded Chicken & Refried Bean Burritos

I can't even tell you how much I love burritos, but whenever I buy them at a takeout spot they're always way too big. Making them at home means more control! These reasonably-sized burritos won't leave you in a food coma during work and they're so delicious. This is a great way to use up leftover chicken if you have any, and roasting the chicken frees you up to prepare other elements. The trick is cooking the shredded chicken and refried beans together to keep the chicken moist. Enjoy these with your favorite salsas on the side!

Prep Time: 10 minutes | Cook Time: 30 minutes | Servings: 4

1 tbsp (15 ml) olive oil

12 oz (336 g) chicken breast, chopped into big pieces

1½ cups (270 g) salsa, plus more for serving

1½ tsp (4 g) salt, divided, plus more to taste

1 tsp ground pepper, divided, plus more to taste

1 tsp olive oil

½ cup (80 g) chopped yellow onion (about ½ an onion)

1 tsp tomato paste

¾ cup (150 g) rice

½ tsp cumin

1½ cups (360 ml) water

1 cup (180 g) refried beans

⅓ cup (80 ml) chicken broth or water

4 large (10-inch [25-cm]) burrito tortillas

1 cup (16 g) chopped cilantro

1⅓ cups (148 g) shredded Mexican blend cheese, or any cheese you'd like

Heat a Dutch oven or large skillet with deep sides over medium heat for a minute or two. Add the olive oil and let it warm up for another minute. Add the chicken breast and salsa with half of the salt and pepper. Bring the heat up so the salsa bubbles gently, and then cook the chicken over low heat, covered, for 25 to 30 minutes, until it's cooked through.

While the chicken cooks, prepare the rice. Add the olive oil and onion to a pot over medium heat. Sauté the onion, stirring often, for about 5 minutes or until fragrant. Stir in the tomato paste, and then add the rice, cumin and the remaining salt and pepper. Stir to combine, then pour in the water. Bring the pot to a boil, then reduce to a simmer and cover with a tight-fitting lid. After 10 minutes, turn the heat off and let the rice steam for at least 10 minutes.

Remove the cooked chicken from the pan and shred it with two forks or chop it into small pieces. Add it back to the pan over medium heat along with the refried beans and chicken broth. Mix well to incorporate the refried beans with the salsa chicken. Let it cook for 5 to 10 minutes, or until the mixture is gently bubbling. Add salt and pepper to taste if desired, and then remove the pan from the heat.

Lay a tortilla on a flat surface. Spread one-fourth of the rice in a horizontal rectangle in the lower third of the tortilla. Imagine that it's like the outline for your burrito. Add one-fourth of the remaining salsa on top of the rice, followed by one-fourth of the cilantro, and then one-fourth of the chicken and refried bean mixture. Lastly, add one-fourth of the shredded cheese.

(continued)

To roll the burrito, fold the bottom of the tortilla above the fillings as far as it will go, and tuck in the two sides of the tortilla over the bottom flap and sides of the fillings. Carefully roll the burrito away from you, keeping the two sides tucked in. Place the burrito seam-side down on a plate while you repeat the last two steps for the remaining three burritos. It can help to watch a video of the rolling process online if you're more of a visual learner!

Wrap the burritos in foil and store in the fridge or freezer until ready to eat. Keep extra salsa on the side!

Storage, Reheating and Serving Notes: These burritos can last in the fridge for up to 5 days and in the freezer for 6 months. To reheat them, you can remove the foil and wrap them in a dry paper towel before sticking them in the microwave. This helps soak up extra moisture and avoid soggy wraps. You can also stick burritos in the oven or toaster oven to reheat and get them crispier on the outside. You can use these methods with frozen burritos as well, but it will take longer. Enjoy with salsa on the side or any other burrito sides you prefer!

Roasted Chickpea, Avocado & Sweet Potato Wraps

What makes the perfect wrap? It's all about having a variety of textures. I've been perfecting lunch wraps for years, and this is "the best one ever" according to my partner. I promise these won't get soggy on you either! Here, we have sweet smokey sweet potatoes, roasted chickpeas lightly mashed, creamy avocado and crunchy kale and radishes. What takes the flavors in this wrap to the next level is the citrus worked into the chickpeas and avocado. You can eat this wrap cold or at room temperature, making it perfect for lunch-on-the-go.

Prep Time: 15 minutes | Cook Time: 40 minutes | Servings: 3

1 sweet potato, chopped into thick fries

2 tbsp (30 ml) olive oil, divided

1 tsp cinnamon

1 tsp cumin

½ tsp salt, plus more to taste

¼ tsp ground pepper, plus more to taste

1 (15-oz [420-ml]) can chickpeas, rinsed and drained

1 tsp paprika

1 tsp curry powder

3 cups (268 g) chopped kale

1 large avocado, pitted

1 tbsp (15 ml) lemon juice, divided

3 large 10-inch (25-cm) tortillas

1 cup (232 g) hummus

6 radishes, halved and sliced

Preheat your oven to 425°F (220°C).

To a mixing bowl, add the sweet potato, 1 tablespoon (15 ml) of olive oil, cinnamon, cumin, salt and pepper. Mix well with a wooden spoon or your hands. Pour the sweet potato onto a baking sheet and spread out the "fries" so they're not touching each other. Bake for 30 to 35 minutes on a lower rack, flipping halfway, until the "fries" are tender and have darkened in color on the outside.

To the same bowl you used before, add the chickpeas, remaining olive oil, paprika, curry powder and salt to taste. Pepper is optional. Mix with a wooden spoon so the chickpeas are coated in the spices. Pour the chickpeas onto another baking sheet and bake for 15 to 20 minutes on a middle or upper rack. They'll be a little crispy and darker in color when they're finished.

Let the sweet potato and chickpeas cool down to room temperature when finished.

Meanwhile, bring 4 to 5 cups (946 ml to 1.2 L) of water to boil and add a few big pinches of salt. Get a bowl of very cold water—it's best if you can add a few ice cubes—ready to go next to the stove. When the water is boiling, carefully add the chopped kale and let it cook for 1 to 2 minutes, until it's vibrantly green. Drain the water from the pot using a strainer and transfer the kale to the bowl of cold water. This stops it from cooking more. Lay a clean kitchen towel on the counter and spread the blanched kale on it to dry before assembling your wraps.

Mash the avocado in a bowl. Add half of the lemon juice and a pinch of salt, and then mix. In another bowl, mash the cooked chickpeas gently. Add the remaining lemon juice and mix.

(continued)

Note: If you're using gluten-free wraps, store the filling and tortillas separately and wrap right before you eat. Gluten-free tortillas tend to break when stored overnight as a wrap.

Let's wrap! Lay a tortilla down on a flat clean surface. Spread one-third of the hummus on the lower third of the wrap horizontally, in the shape you want your wrap to be in. Think of it like you're "outlining" the shape of your wrap with the hummus. Place one-third of the kale on the hummus, followed by an even layer of sweet potatoes—make sure they're not piled on top of each other! Add one-third of the mashed avocado on the potatoes, followed by one-third of the lightly mashed chickpeas. Top it off with a layer of sliced radishes.

With your hands on either side of the wrap, fold the bottom of the wrap over the filling—it's okay if it doesn't cover the filling completely. Then fold the two sides over the edges of the filling. This is the tricky part—with the sides folded in, fold the wrap and filling completely over away from you. Adjust to tuck in the sides and keep rolling until you're out of tortilla. This takes practice! Repeat the last two steps two more times to make all three wraps.

Storage, Reheating and Serving Notes: These wraps can last in the fridge for up to 4 days and they're not freezer friendly. Store in an airtight container in the fridge until you're ready to eat! These can be eaten cold, room temperature or warmed in the microwave or on the stove.

Kimchi Mushroom Quesadillas

Have you ever tried kimchi with cheese? This is one of my favorite combinations. Kimchi and cheese are a match made in heaven and I have the quesadillas to prove it! If you want to add meat to these, they're also great with ground beef or leftover chopped steak. The green bell pepper adds an excellent crunch and the kimchi brings a lot of flavor!

Prep Time: 10 minutes | Cook Time: 30 minutes | Servings: 3

Cooking spray

1 tbsp (15 ml) olive oil

4 scallions, white and green ends chopped and separated

8 oz (226 g) baby bella mushrooms, sliced

1 green bell pepper, chopped

½ tsp salt

¼ tsp ground pepper

1 cup (33 g) roughly chopped spinach

3 large 10-inch (25-cm) tortillas

1 (8-oz [226-g]) bag shredded cheddar cheese

1 cup (170 g) kimchi

Salsa, for serving

Preheat your oven to 375°F (190°C). Prepare a baking sheet with cooking spray.

Warm up a skillet over medium heat for a minute or two, then add the olive oil. Add the white ends of the scallions, mushrooms, bell pepper, salt and pepper. Cook over medium heat for about 10 minutes, stirring occasionally, until the mushrooms have reduced in size and are fragrant. Turn off the heat and stir in the spinach. Cover the pan to let the spinach steam for 3 to 5 minutes.

Lay a tortilla on a flat surface. Add ⅓ cup (37 g) of the cheese and spread it on half of the tortilla. On top of the cheese, add a layer of one-third of the kimchi, then add a layer of one-third of the mushroom mixture. Sprinkle on one-third of the green ends of the scallions, then add ⅓ cup (37 g) of cheese on top in a layer. Fold the empty side of the tortilla on top of the fillings and press down gently to even the fillings out. Place the quesadilla on the sheet pan. Repeat this with two more tortillas.

Bake the quesadillas for 15 to 20 minutes, until the cheese has melted and the tortillas are slightly brown in color. If you want, you can flip the quesadillas and continue to bake for 5 more minutes.

Let the quesadillas cool completely before slicing them into thirds and placing them in meal prep containers. You can separate the pieces with parchment paper to avoid sogginess. Keep the salsa and any additional toppings on the side.

Storage, Reheating and Serving Notes: These quesadillas can last for up to 4 days in the fridge and 6 months in the freezer. The best way to reheat this meal is in the microwave for a minute, then in a toaster oven. You can also reheat it in the oven—I like to broil it—or on the stove. The extra step of reheating it in a toaster or oven helps it get crispy again! Enjoy this with your favorite salsa on the side.

Black Bean, Spinach & Pesto Quesadillas

There are a lot of flavors happening in this quesadilla, but it's worth it. Black beans add a good amount of protein and an interesting texture, plus they pair well with the pesto, olives, tomatoes and not one, but two types of cheese! Make sure to wait until they're fully cool before slicing and storing in the fridge for best results.

Prep Time: 10 minutes | Cook Time: 30 minutes | Servings: 3

Cooking spray

1 tbsp (15 ml) olive oil

½ cup (80 g) chopped yellow onion (about ½ an onion)

1 (15-oz [420-ml]) can black beans, rinsed and drained

½ tsp salt

¼ tsp ground pepper

1 tsp oregano

3 cups (100 g) roughly chopped spinach

1 (8-oz [226-g]) bag shredded mozzarella

3 large (10-inch [25-cm]) tortillas

1 cup (150 g) crumbled feta cheese

⅔ cup (96 g) pesto

½ cup (90 g) Kalamata olives, halved

2 cups (108 g) sun-dried tomatoes, chopped

Preheat your oven to 375°F (190°C). Prepare a baking sheet with cooking spray.

Warm up a skillet over medium heat for a minute, then add the olive oil. After a minute or two, add the yellow onion and let it cook for 5 minutes, stirring occasionally, until fragrant. Add the black beans with salt, pepper and oregano. Cook for 10 minutes, stirring occasionally, until they've softened. Turn off the heat and stir in the spinach and mozzarella cheese. Cover the pan and let the spinach steam for 3 to 5 minutes.

Lay a tortilla on a flat surface. Sprinkle ⅓ cup (37 g) of mozzarella cheese on half of the tortilla in an even layer. Top with one-third of the feta. Add one-third of the black bean–spinach mixture on top of the cheese. Spread one-third of the pesto on top of the black bean layer. Add one third of the olives and sun-dried tomatoes in the next layer. Top with ⅓ cup (37 g) of mozzarella cheese and fold the empty side of the tortilla over the side with the fillings. Press down gently to even the fillings out. Place the quesadilla on the baking sheet and repeat this process two more times.

Bake the quesadillas for 15 to 20 minutes, until the cheese has melted and the tortillas are slightly brown in color. If you want, you can flip the quesadillas and continue to bake for 5 more minutes.

Let the quesadillas cool completely before slicing them into thirds and placing them in meal prep containers. You can separate the pieces with parchment paper to avoid sogginess.

Storage, Reheating and Serving Notes: These quesadillas can last for up to 4 days in the fridge and 6 months in the freezer. Reheat this meal in the microwave for a minute, then in the toaster oven. You can also reheat it in the oven—I like to broil it—or on the stove. Reheating it in a toaster or oven helps it get crispy again! Enjoy this with your favorite tomato-based salsa on the side.

Buffalo Chicken Tacos

Whenever I get a craving for a buffalo-flavored something, which is about once a month, these are my go-to. The only thing you have to cook is the buffalo chicken! You can easily transform these elements into a salad, sheet pan pizza, quesadilla, burrito or even a baked pasta dish if you don't want to eat tacos for a few days in a row. To turn this meal into a baked pasta dish, toss the taco fillings, except for the lettuce, with cooked pasta and a quick cheese sauce, and then bake!

Prep Time: 15 minutes | Cook Time: 30 minutes | Servings: 3

FOR THE CHICKEN

1 tbsp (15 ml) olive oil

1 lb (454 g) chicken breast, chopped into big pieces

½ tsp salt

¼ tsp ground pepper

2 tbsp (28 g) butter

2 cloves garlic, minced

¼ cup (60 ml) chicken broth (sub water)

½ cup (120 ml) hot sauce (I use Frank's® Hot Sauce)

FOR THE SALSA

½ cup (80 g) finely chopped red onion (about ½ an onion)

⅔ cup (98 g) cherry tomatoes, chopped small

2 scallions, green ends chopped

1 avocado, chopped

1 lime, juiced

FOR ASSEMBLING THE TACOS

¾ cup (180 ml) ranch, for serving, optional

6–9 small (6-inch [15-cm]) tortillas

3 cups (216 g) chopped lettuce, washed

Heat a medium or large skillet for 2 to 3 minutes over medium heat. Add the olive oil and let it warm up for a minute. Meanwhile, pat the chicken breast dry and season one side with half of the salt and pepper. Place the seasoned side down on the pan, and then add the remaining salt and pepper to the unseasoned side once it's in the pan. Cook on each side over medium heat for 5 to 6 minutes. Remove it from the pan when it's fully cooked through—the chicken should be firm to the touch and a meat thermometer will read 165°F (74°C)—and let it rest for 10 to 15 minutes.

While the chicken rests, make the salsa. Toss the chopped red onion, tomatoes, scallions, avocado and juice from one lime together in a small bowl. Set aside.

To the same skillet you used before, add the butter, garlic, chicken broth and hot sauce. Let the butter melt and stir everything together. Bring the mixture to a simmer so it thickens slightly.

After the chicken has rested, shred it with two forks. Add it to the pan with the hot sauce mixture over medium heat and toss until it's well coated.

Store the chicken, salsa, lettuce, ranch and tortillas separately. If you want to divide the ingredients among meal prep containers, I suggest using a container with dividers to keep the elements separate, especially the chicken, lettuce and salsa. When you're ready to eat, assemble the tacos by spreading ranch on the tortillas, followed by the lettuce, buffalo chicken, salsa and more ranch.

Storage, Reheating and Serving Notes: These tacos will last in the fridge for up to 4 days. You can eat them cold or at room temperature. Alternatively, you can reheat just the chicken in the microwave or on the stove and warm the tortillas before eating.

Orange-Marinated Steak Fajitas

This is one of my all-time favorite meals to prepare for work lunches! It instantly transports me to a summer cookout even if I'm swamped at my desk, trying to eat quickly between meetings. You can easily swap out steak for chicken, shrimp or tempeh.

Prep Time: 10 minutes | Cook Time: 25 minutes | Servings: 3

FOR THE STEAK

1 navel orange, halved

½ tbsp (4 g) taco seasoning, divided

1 tsp cumin

½ tsp salt

Pepper to taste

1 lime

1½ tbsp (3 ml) olive oil

1 lb (454 g) flank steak or skirt steak

FOR EVERYTHING ELSE

½ tbsp (4g) taco seasoning

1 red bell pepper, sliced

1 green bell pepper, sliced

1 yellow bell pepper, sliced

1 medium yellow onion, sliced

1½ tbsp (23 ml) olive oil

½ tsp salt

¼ tsp ground pepper

1 tbsp (15 ml) vegetable oil

6 small (6-inch [15-cm]) tortillas

½ cup (8 g) chopped cilantro, for garnish, optional

1 lime, cut into wedges

Preheat your oven to 425°F (220°C).

Add the juice from an orange, half of the taco seasoning, cumin, salt, pepper, juice from one lime and half of the olive oil in a measuring glass. Mix well. Add the steak and marinade to a ziplock bag. Turn the bag over a few times to fully coat the steak, then let it sit on the counter for 15 to 60 minutes. Note that you can do this step 24 hours ahead and let the steak marinate in the fridge.

Toss the sliced bell peppers and onion in a bowl with the remaining taco seasoning and olive oil. Add the salt and pepper. Toss well, then transfer the mixture to a baking sheet. Make sure to spread the veggies out so they aren't overlapping too much. Bake for 15 to 20 minutes, stirring and flipping the mixture halfway through cooktime. To get them to look more charred, you can broil the peppers and onion for a minute or two.

When you're ready to cook the steak, let it sit at room temperature for a few minutes if it was in the fridge. Meanwhile, preheat a cast-iron or stainless steel skillet for a few minutes. It should be very hot. Add the vegetable oil to the pan, and then remove the steak from the marinade and carefully place it in the pan. Let it cook for 5 minutes over medium-high heat, and then flip it over and continue cooking for another 3 to 4 minutes, or longer for a thicker cut. When finished, it should be firm to the touch but give slightly. A meat thermometer will read 125°F (52°C) for a medium-rare steak when it's ready to come off the pan. Let the steak rest for at least 15 minutes before slicing.

Divide the bell peppers and sliced steak among three meal prep containers. Keep the tortillas on the side until ready to eat. Garnish with cilantro if you wish. Cut the remaining lime and add the wedges to each container.

Storage, Reheating and Serving Notes: These fajitas will last in the fridge for up to 4 days. I recommend removing the lime wedges, and then reheating them in the microwave or on the stove. Warm up the fajita tortillas, too, if you can! Squeeze the lime wedge over the steak before eating.

BUFFET MEAL PREP

Meal prepping lunches for work doesn't have to involve making full recipes with a main and sides, like most of the recipes in this book. You can absolutely prep meal elements ahead to assemble as needed. This method of prep, called "buffet meal prep," is perfect if you have a more unpredictable schedule or need more variety in your food. Instead of prepping complete meals, you're prepping standalone ingredients to turn into something different based on your food mood. This type of prep requires more work in the moment before you eat, but again, it's ideal if you have less time on weekends to cook and want to avoid repetition in meals.

I recommend storing each meal element separately in glass container for up to 5 days in the fridge. Plastic works, too, but in my experience, glass is optimal for keeping foods fresh. Plus, there's less risk of staining the container.

Meal Combinations for Buffet Meal Prep

Here are some ways that I suggest you combine the recipes in this chapter to make full, exciting meals. The ingredients in italics are extras that you can throw in to make these meals complete. These ideas are basic, but as you keep up your meal prep routine, you'll find more ways to creatively put these elements together.

- Roasted chicken + roasted vegetables + hummus + *a tortilla* = lunch wraps
- Roasted chicken, tofu or salmon + coconut rice + *leftover veggies* + *egg* = fried rice
- Salmon + roasted vegetables + green rice + tahini sauce = salmon bowl
- Tofu + mango salsa + coconut rice + herb sauce = mango rice bowl
- Salmon, tofu or chicken + pickled onions + mango salsa + *taco tortillas* = tacos
- Tofu + roasted vegetables + hummus + *a tortilla* = vegan lunch wraps
- Tofu + green rice + roasted vegetables + *egg* = fried rice
- Roast chicken + salsa rice + quick pickled onions + *beans* + *tortilla* = burritos

Rice Three Ways

Rice is my favorite carb element for meal prep! You can buy so much of it in bulk and change up the flavors so easily with just a few tweaks. Rice can last in the fridge for a while, can be frozen and reheats easily, if you know the trick—see below!

Green Rice

This green rice recipe involves cooking rice with cilantro and milk, resulting in a luxurious, creamy and flavorful base for your weekly meal preps. Traditionally, to make green rice, you'd blend cilantro, garlic, milk and other ingredients in a food processor to use as the cooking liquid for the rice, but we're skipping that step to make it a bit faster! I love using green rice as a base for roasted vegetables and baked or grilled proteins.

Prep Time: 5 minutes | Cook Time: 20 minutes | Makes: 1½ cups (286 g)

¾ cup (150 g) rice
1 tsp olive oil
1 clove garlic, minced
½ tsp salt
1 cup (16 g) cilantro
1 cup (240 ml) chicken broth
½ cup (120 ml) milk

Add the rice, olive oil, garlic, salt and cilantro to a pot over medium heat. Stir everything together and cook for a minute. Then add the chicken broth and milk. Bring the mixture to a boil, and then cover and reduce the heat to a simmer. Cook for 10 minutes, then remove the pot from the heat and let the rice steam for at least 10 more minutes before fluffing with a fork.

Transfer the rice to a large airtight container and store in the fridge.

Storage and Reheating Notes: Cooked rice can last in the fridge for up to 6 days and can be frozen for 6 months. It reheats well in the microwave or on the stove when you add a little water to it and cover it partially so it can steam back to life. Frozen rice can be reheated in the microwave or on the stove with 2 tablespoons (30 ml) of water for a few minutes.

(continued)

Salsa Rice

Replacing some of your cooking liquid with salsa is such an easy way to switch up regular rice! You can use any kind of tomato-based salsa for this recipe, which gives it a red color and tons of flavor. I recommend using salsa rice in burritos and burrito bowls!

Prep Time: 5 minutes | Cook Time: 20 minutes | Makes: 1½ cups (286 g)

¾ cup (150 g) rice
1 cup (180 g) salsa
½ cup (120 ml) water
¼ tsp salt

Add the rice, salsa, water and salt to a pot over medium heat. Stir everything together and cook for a minute and bring the mixture to a boil, and then cover the pot and reduce the heat to a simmer. Cook for 10 minutes, and then remove the pot from the heat and let the rice steam for at least 10 more minutes before fluffing with a fork.

Transfer the rice to a large airtight container and store in the fridge.

Storage and Reheating Notes: Cooked rice can last in the fridge for up to 6 days and can be frozen for 6 months. It reheats well in the microwave or on the stove when you add a little water to it and cover it partially so it can steam back to life. Frozen rice can be reheated in the microwave or on the stove with 2 tablespoons (30 ml) of water for a few minutes.

Coconut Rice

Another way to transform rice is by replacing some of the liquid with canned coconut milk. This rice will have a sweeter flavor and stickier texture, making it great for Asian-inspired bowls and fried rice dishes.

Prep Time: 5 minutes | Cook Time: 20 minutes | Makes: 1½ cups (286 g)

¾ cup (150 g) rice
1 cup (240 ml) coconut milk
½ cup (120 ml) water
½ tsp salt

Add the rice, coconut milk, water and salt to a pot over medium heat. Stir everything together and cook for a minute and bring the mixture to a boil, and then cover the pot and reduce the heat to a simmer. Cook for 10 minutes, and then remove the pot from the heat and let the rice steam for at least 10 more minutes before fluffing with a fork.

Transfer the rice to a large airtight container and store in the fridge.

Storage and Reheating Notes: Cooked rice can last in the fridge for up to 6 days and can be frozen for 6 months. It reheats well in the microwave or on the stove when you add a little water to it and cover it partially so it can steam back to life. Frozen rice can be reheated in the microwave or on the stove with 2 tablespoons (30 ml) of water for a few minutes.

Shortcut Roasted Chicken

Instead of roasting a whole chicken, which takes a lot longer, you can get a similar effect by roasting a pound of chicken—any cuts will work for this recipe—with herbs, paprika and lemon, and then using it throughout the week. Shred this chicken for tacos, salads, wraps or just to pair with rice and some roasted veggies. Having this on hand makes lunches a lot easier to assemble if you're not quite sure what you're in the mood for!

Prep Time: 10 minutes | Cook Time: 30 minutes | Servings: 3

1 lb (454 g) chicken (can be thighs, breasts and/or drumsticks)

1½ tbsp (23 ml) olive oil

½ tsp paprika

1 tbsp (2 g) chopped mixed herbs (I used parsley, dill and rosemary)

4 cloves garlic, minced

Salt and pepper to taste

1 lemon, quartered

Preheat your oven to 400°F (200°C).

Place the chicken in a bowl and add the olive oil, paprika, herbs, garlic, salt and pepper. Toss well, and then add the chicken to a baking dish or a sheet pan. Tuck lemon quarters under the chicken.

If using chicken breasts only, roast for 20 to 25 minutes. If using chicken thighs or drumsticks, roast for 25 to 30 minutes. No matter which cut you use, roast until the chicken is firm to the touch. If using a meat thermometer, the internal temperature should read 165°F (73°C). Let the chicken rest for at least 15 minutes before slicing, shredding or chopping. You can leave the chicken whole as well.

When the chicken is cool, transfer to a large airtight container and store in the fridge.

Storage, Reheating and Serving Notes: This chicken can last in the fridge for up to 5 days. I don't recommend freezing it. It's best reheated on the stove, in the oven or in the microwave. To avoid overcooking it, keep the heat or power lower when reheating.

Sheet Pan Roasted Vegetables

If there's anything to meal prep for work lunches, it's roasted vegetables. You will not be sorry during the week when you have these ready-to-eat veggies on hand for any quick meal you're in the mood for. After meal prepping for several years, here's the truth: Roasted vegetables don't stay crispy after a night or two in the fridge. That's why I recommend pairing them with our Green Rice (page 146), or any leftover quinoa or pasta to soak up that extra moisture.

Prep Time: 10 minutes | Cook Time: 40 minutes | Servings: 3

7 oz (198 g) broccoli, chopped into florets

2 medium carrots, chopped

1 large red bell pepper, chopped

1–2 (162 g) leeks, white ends sliced and green ends discarded

2 tbsp (30 ml) olive oil

Salt and pepper to taste

1 tsp garlic powder

Preheat your oven to 400°F (200°C).

Add the broccoli, carrots, bell pepper, leeks, olive oil, salt, pepper and garlic powder to a bowl. Toss everything together, and then pour the vegetables onto a baking sheet. Make sure to spread the vegetables out so they have enough space. Roast for 20 to 25 minutes, flipping halfway through the roasting process, until the carrots are fork-tender.

Let the vegetables cool completely on the sheet pan, and then transfer them to a large container and store in the fridge.

Storage and Reheating Notes: Roasted veggies will never stay crispy after being stored in the fridge, unless you reheat them under the broiler in the oven or with an air fryer. You can reheat roasted veggies in the microwave, on the stove or in the toaster oven.

Baked Mustard Lemon Dill Salmon

Aside from the soy honey baked salmon in our Crunchy Mandarin Salad recipe (page 89), this is my other favorite way to prepare baked salmon. It goes with just about any meal and yes, reheats well thanks to the flavors. The key to reheating salmon properly is not overcooking it initially—I recommend a meat thermometer here—and jazzing it up with flavor! But if you prefer to only prep salmon for meals at home to avoid potentially stinking up your office kitchen, we get it. Either way, this versatile protein source will keep you energized throughout the week, especially when you don't feel like cooking.

Prep Time: 5 minutes | Cook Time 20 minutes | Servings: 3

1 lemon
2 tbsp (30 ml) olive oil, divided
1 tbsp (15 ml) Dijon mustard
3 cloves garlic, minced
2 tbsp (6 g) chopped dill
1 lb (454 g) salmon fillet

Preheat your oven to 400°F (200°C). Cut the lemon in half. Juice one half (1 tablespoon [15 ml]) and cut the remaining half into three lemon slices.

Add 1 tablespoon (15 ml) of the olive oil, Dijon mustard, garlic, lemon juice and dill to a measuring glass. Stir to combine and then set aside.

Use the remaining olive oil to grease a sheet pan or baking sheet. Place the salmon on the greased dish or sheet. Pour the mustard mixture onto the salmon. Use a brush or spoon to collect extra sauce that drips off the salmon and drizzle it back on top. Place the three lemon slices on top of the salmon, taking care not to overlap them. Bake for 20 minutes, or until the edges of the salmon have darkened in color and it's firm to the touch and flakes apart. If using a meat thermometer, the internal temperature of the thickest part of the salmon should be 140 to 145° F (60 to 63°C).

Let the salmon cool and then cut into pieces as needed. Store in an airtight container in the fridge.

Storage and Reheating Notes: Salmon can last in the fridge for up to 4 days. I don't recommend freezing it. Remove lemon wedges before reheating. It's best reheated on the stove, in the oven or in the microwave. To avoid overcooking it, keep the heat or power lower when reheating. You can also enjoy this roasted salmon cold or room temperature! You can use this salmon as a main or chop it up to put on top of salads, grain bowls or use in wraps.

Soy Honey Tofu

Tofu is the first protein I truly learned to master and this is my favorite way to prepare it! I know it can be intimidating, but I promise it's easy. It has a lovely sweet and savory flavor, and a firm and satisfying texture that can go with almost any meal. Use this baked tofu on salads, in wraps, over rice or with noodle dishes. I recommend always using firm tofu for best results!

Prep Time: 25 minutes | Cook Time: 25 minutes | Servings: 3

Cooking spray
1 (14-oz [392-ml]) package firm tofu, drained
1 clove garlic, minced
1-inch (2.5-cm) piece ginger, grated
⅓ cup (80 ml) honey
⅓ cup (80 ml) soy sauce
1 tbsp (15 ml) rice vinegar

Preheat your oven to 400°F (200°C). Prepare a baking sheet with cooking spray.

To press the tofu, wrap it in a paper towel or clean kitchen towel and set it on a plate. Place something heavy on top of the tofu—I use my cast-iron skillet or heavy cookbooks. Let the tofu press for 10 to 20 minutes, and then unwrap it and chop it into cubes.

While the tofu presses, add the garlic, ginger, honey, soy sauce and rice vinegar to a measuring glass. Stir well to combine.

Add the pressed tofu to a ziplock bag or baking dish and pour the marinade on top. Gently toss the tofu in the marinade and let it sit for 10 to 15 minutes at room temperature.

Using a slotted spoon, transfer the tofu to the sheet pan and bake for 20 to 25 minutes, flipping halfway through the baking process. The tofu should be darker around the edges and firm to the touch when finished. To make the tofu even firmer, bake for another 10 minutes at 375°F (190°C).

Transfer the tofu to a large container and store in the fridge after it has cooled slightly.

Storage, Reheating and Serving Notes: Soy Honey Tofu can last in the fridge for up to 6 days. You can enjoy it with meals cold, at room temperature or reheated on the stove, in the oven or in the microwave.

LUNCH-SAVING TOPPINGS

Sometimes, when we're not in the mood for what we meal prepped, it just needs a little something extra to feel new and fresh again—that's what lunch savers are. These are all my favorite dressings, sauces, condiments and additions to meals that make them feel new again.

If you're feeling super drained, usually a fresh sprinkle of cheese or chopped cilantro can be enough to revive a meal. But these recipes can all be prepped ahead and can last in the fridge for over a week in airtight jars and containers.

It's best to keep recipes like the Creamy Avocado Herb Sauce (page 160) and the All-Purpose Tahini Lemon Sauce (page 163) on the side. But My Go-To Hummus (page 167) and the Quick Pickled Red Onions (page 168) can actually be reheated with your meals if you'd like.

I recommend keeping some smaller containers and jars around for storing lunch savers. My favorite containers for these are 16-oz (454-ml) mason jars which are easy to keep organized in the fridge. But to take small amounts of these on the go, you'll need smaller containers. The best, in my opinion, are the plastic 4-ounce (113-ml) containers you can usually find in the grocery store. They don't have snap lids, but are pretty reliable for dressings and sauces to be kept on the side for meal preps.

Creamy Avocado Herb Sauce

I make this thick, creamy sauce religiously every week. It's the best way to use up avocados and herbs on their last legs and there are endless ways to customize it! You can use tahini, sour cream or mayonnaise instead of yogurt. You can add nuts for a more pesto-like texture or use spinach instead of herbs for a different flavor. Any herbs work for this sauce. This recipe goes well with our Jerk Shrimp, Corn & Black Bean Salad (page 86), Chipotle Black Bean Avocado Quinoa Salad (page 54) and the Chicken Kahti Roll–Inspired Bowls (page 68).

Prep Time: 5 minutes | Cook time: 0 minutes | Makes: 1 cup (240 ml)

2 cups (32 g) of fresh mixed herb leaves (basil, cilantro, parsley, mint, dill all work)

1 tbsp (15 ml) olive oil

¼ cup (60 ml) lemon juice or lime juice

½ large avocado (83 g)

2 tbsp (30 ml) plain yogurt or sour cream or tahini

2 tbsp (30 ml) water, plus more as needed

Salt and pepper to taste

Add the herbs to a food processor and process until they're finely chopped. Add the olive oil, lemon juice, avocado, yogurt, water, salt and pepper to the processor and process until you have a smooth, creamy sauce. Add more water 1 tablespoon (15 ml) at a time to thin if you'd like!

Storage Notes: This herby sauce lasts in the fridge for 5 days! It's best at room temperature or cold. It's not freezer friendly.

All-Purpose Tahini Lemon Sauce

Tahini is a ground sesame seed spread that's super versatile, and it makes a great base for dairy-free sauces and dressing. This all-purpose sauce can be used on green salads, grain salads, bowl meals and even with pasta. I love it in wraps too. Its creamy texture and subtle nutty flavor can make any meal feel a bit fancier. This sauce would be perfect on the Butternut Squash Chickpea Kale Salad (page 80), Roasted Chickpea, Avocado & Sweet Potato Wrap (page 133) and the Chickpea Halloumi Farro Bowl (page 71).

Prep Time: 5 minutes | Cook Time: 0 minutes | Makes: ¾ cup (180 ml)

⅓ cup (80 ml) tahini

3 tbsp (45 ml) lemon juice

1 tbsp (15 ml) olive oil

3 tbsp (45 ml) room-temperature water

Salt to taste, pepper optional

To a jar or measuring glass, add the tahini, lemon juice, olive oil, water, salt and pepper, if using. Use a fork to stir well. Taste the sauce and adjust flavors to your preference. You may want to add more lemon juice or water to thin the sauce, as it does tend to thicken in the fridge.

Storage Notes: This tahini sauce lasts in the fridge for up to 10 days. It's best at room temperature or cold and isn't freezer friendly.

Mango Jalapeño Salsa

I'm a big fan of making fruit salsa at home. This mango salsa goes with just about anything— on top of burgers, on tacos, in wraps, with stir-fries or over rice. You can swap mangoes out for apples, pears, peaches or pineapples—I've tried them all and they're great. I recommend using this salsa with the Honey Chipotle Shrimp Quinoa Bowls (page 72), the Salmon & Sweet Potato Sheet Pan (page 36) and as a fun twist on our Orange-Marinated Steak Fajitas (page 142). This salsa really brightens up any meal!

Prep Time: 10 minutes | Cook Time: 0 minutes | Makes: 1 cup (240 ml)

1 large red bell pepper, chopped

1 mango, chopped

1 jalapeño, seeded and chopped

½ tsp salt, plus more to taste

½ cup (8 g) chopped cilantro

1 lime, for juices

¼ tsp cayenne or crushed red pepper, optional

Toss the bell pepper, mango and jalapeño in a bowl with the salt. Add the cilantro and squeeze lime juice over the mixture and add cayenne if desired, and then toss again. Taste and adjust the salt to your preference.

Storage Notes: This salsa can last in the fridge for 6 days. It's great cold, room temperature or even warmed up.

My Go-To Hummus

It's a fact that homemade hummus tastes better than store bought. Plus, it's cheaper to make in the long run and you can customize it however you want! You can even freeze it if you want to double this recipe to always have some on hand. I love having hummus around for wraps like our Roasted Chickpea, Avocado & Sweet Potato Wraps on page 133, snacking and even to blend into pasta sauces, depending on the dish.

Prep Time: 5 minutes | Cook Time: 0 minutes | Makes: 2 cups (480 ml)

1 (15-oz [420-ml]) can chickpeas, drained

⅓ cup (80 ml) tahini

½ tsp salt

Pepper to taste

3 tbsp (45 ml) water, plus more to thin if desired

1 tbsp (15 ml) lemon juice

1 tbsp (15 ml) olive oil

½ tsp paprika

½ tsp cumin

Add the chickpeas, tahini, salt, pepper, water, lemon juice, olive oil, paprika and cumin to a food processor. Process for about 2 minutes, scraping down the sides of the processor as needed. To thin the hummus, add 1 tablespoon (15 ml) of water at a time until you've reached your desired consistency. Transfer the hummus to an airtight container and store in the fridge.

Storage Notes: Homemade hummus can last for up to 2 weeks in the fridge and 6 months in the freezer. Thaw frozen hummus out in the fridge overnight to enjoy with crackers, crudites, in wraps or on its own!

Quick Pickled Red Onions

There's always a jar of these pickled red onions in my fridge. I love using them on tacos and in wraps, but I especially love to use them to refresh any lunch option that needs a bit of color and something super flavorful. Sometimes that pop of pink is all a meal needs to feel like new! Add these to the Chicken Kahti Roll–Inspired Bowls (page 68), the Buffalo Chicken Tacos (page 141) or on top of the Chipotle Black Bean Avocado Quinoa Salad (page 54).

Prep Time: 5 minutes | Cook Time: 5 minutes | Makes: 1 lb (143 ml)

½ cup (120 ml) apple cider vinegar

½ cup (120 ml) water

¼ cup (50 g) sugar

2 tsp (12 g) salt

1 clove garlic, minced

¼ tsp crushed red pepper, optional

1 medium red onion, sliced thin

To a measuring glass, add the apple cider vinegar, water, sugar, salt, minced garlic and crushed red pepper, if using. If you have a microwave, heat the mixture for 90 seconds. Alternatively, you can pour the mixture into a small pot and heat it on medium heat for 2 to 3 minutes, or until the salt and sugar have dissolved. Then remove from the heat.

Add the onion to a mason jar or glass container. Pour the vinegar mixture over the onions and using a spoon, push the onions down to submerge them completely. Leave the container uncovered until it's completely cool, and then cover and store in the fridge.

Storage Notes: Quick Pickled Red Onions are good in the fridge for 3 weeks. They're not freezer friendly. They can be enjoyed cold, at room temperature or heated up with a meal, but they're best when cold.

ACKNOWLEDGMENTS

Thank YOU so much! My dream of writing a cookbook wouldn't have become a reality without you and the entire Workweek Lunch community. Thank you so much for spreading the love, sharing your meal prep masterpieces on social media and with your friends and family. It means so much to me and the Workweek Lunch team. You're the reason I show up every day and you give the team and me so much inspiration. Your excitement for this book helped me get through it!

Thank you, Daniella Koren, for always believing in me, pushing me and being the best mom/mentor anyone could ask for. This book wouldn't have been a reality without your constant encouragement throughout my business journey.

A huge thank you to Alyssa Lash, Melenie McGregor, Jessica Phillips and Morgan Yiu for the constant positivity, support and encouragement while I wrote this book, on top of helping the company run smoothly during the entire process. You are the dream team!

Thank you Curt Morgan, who taste-tested every single recipe in this book, and ran to the grocery store when I forgot last minute items!

Big thanks to Zoe Vock, Rachel Saslaw, Imani Brammer, Eliza Bailey, Michelle Ammirati and Allison Currier for rooting for me every step of the way, letting me vent to you and helping me brainstorm creative recipe ideas when I got stuck!

So much love for Saba Matthew Kirsch and Alex Koren for being so supportive through this process. Thank you for always rooting for me!

Thanks to Tiffany Dahle and everyone in our food blogger Facebook community who encouraged me to go for it and write this book! Your transparency and willingness to answer questions and provide insight from your experience has been invaluable to me.

Thank you to Morgan Petroski for making me look like a natural in front of the camera in photos for this cookbook.

Thanks to Jenna Fagan and the Page Street Publishing team for making this book a possibility and for working so hard to make it a valuable resource full of delicious work lunches that can reach thousands of home cooks.

Sending all the gratitude and love for all the Workweek Preppers who stepped up to help test these recipes on tight deadlines! Your feedback and notes made this book so much better. You'll never know how much I appreciate your reliability and dedication to helping me make this book the best it could be!

ABOUT THE AUTHOR

Talia Koren is the founder and CEO of Workweek Lunch, a meal plan subscription service and blog that helps busy people all over the world master meal prep to get more out of life. She has taught meal prep cooking classes in New York City, led meal prep workshops at various companies and has appeared in publications including the *New York Times*, *Women's Health* and *Shape*, sharing her expertise for meal prepping lunches you'll actually look forward to. Talia's Instagram, blog and YouTube channel, Workweek Lunch, reaches hundreds of thousands of dedicated fans and home cooks.

Want even more creative meal prep ideas and helpful resources? Come join the meal prep party here!

www.workweeklunch.com

⊙ @workweeklunch

▶ /workweeklunch

INDEX